BeaR
with
Hope

Hope and Love Always!
♡ *Tammy Hendricks*

Tammy Hendricks

Picosie Publishing
OK USA

Bear with Hope

Tammy Hendricks LLC
© 2016 Picosie Publishing
Printed in the United States of America
Contact Tammy at www.BearWithHope.com

Library of Congress Control Number: 2016946359
ISBN: 9780996978101

FIRST EDITION

Special thanks and recognition to:
Janet Kruskamp
Janetkruskamp.com- fineartamerica.com
Photos of original artwork published with permission from Mary Sher
Bentley Licensing Group
15 Crow Canyon Court, Suite 210
San Ramon, CA 94583
925-208-1302
www.bentleylicensinggroup.com

John Bindon
Photos of original artwork published with permission from John Bindon
Artwork copyright John Bindon all inquiries *jbindon@bindonart.com*

Bear with Hope is for inspirational purposes and not a substitute for therapy. If you
need psychological help please contact a mental health provider, clergy, or other
medical professional who can provide the guidance and help needed.

Some names and identifying characteristics have been
changed to protect the privacy of the individual.

Dedicated to Mama

Contents

Many of us spend our whole lives running from feeling with the mistaken belief that you cannot bear the pain. But you have already borne the pain. What you have not done is feel all you are beyond the pain. —St. Bartholomew

Introduction

This morning, April 23, 2016, seems on the outside like any other spring day in Oklahoma. As usual, I pour my cup of coffee, grab a handful of dog biscuits, and am immediately led out the back door by our four little dogs. We have a large backyard nestled against a beautiful wooded area, which provides just enough seclusion to feel quietness with nature. As with every morning, we start with a walk around the edge of the fence line, hoping to catch a whiff of the squirrel or bunny that was there just hours before. Pico, our fifteen-year-old miniature schnauzer, appreciates and enjoys this tradition as much as I do, relishing the sights and sounds of a new day. Above my head, the Purple Martins are chattering amongst themselves, relentlessly swooping after the morning fireflies in the clear blue sky. At my feet, the morning dew is so heavy, it has dampened my toes even through my house shoes. These are meaningful moments I will treasure for a lifetime.

However, it is not like any other morning.

My mother-in-law is being laid to rest today. She has lost her fight with breast cancer. I have these few minutes alone to reflect on my husband, Marc, his brother and sister, and their journey ahead without her—a journey I started twenty years ago when my own mother lost her battle to breast cancer; one of sadness, pain, even anger, but also one of strength, wisdom, and hope.

I don't know what kind of tough times you are going through, or have been through. Maybe you have had recent hurts and disappointments, or past experiences and pain that won't go away. Perhaps the pain is something that's just always been with you. I don't presume to know how you feel, because I don't—no one knows but you. I only know I've been through some tough times, and I know what it's like to hurt.

Like so many others, I've asked the *why* question, and I've searched for answers. I find some, but others remain elusive, and I can accept this. What I won't accept though, is feeling helpless and hopeless. Instead of dwelling on *why* something has happened, I ask *how*; how can I give this terrible event or situation meaning? How can I use it for good? By replacing the *why* with *how*, the circumstances no longer render us helpless or powerless; but rather we are empowered by them.

Bear with Hope is not a typical self-help book. It is not meant to treat, or advise those with serious mental illness; it is not about psychotherapy, the psychology or stages of grief, nor is it religiously motivated; it matters not our faith, race, color, or culture— hope does not judge nor discriminate. There are wonderful books that delve deeply into those issues, but this isn't one of them. *Bear with Hope* is more practical, conversational, and personal. What you will find are words of encouragement and simple ways to experience joy, even in the midst of struggles or sorrow.

I share individual stories from beautiful people who have shared their struggles, and how they were able to celebrate overcoming. I offer a personal perspective and narrative, forged not only from my experience as a mental health professional, but also from overcoming the challenges of a physical disability from birth, infertility, divorce, and my mother's death after a long and painful battle with breast cancer.

Your tough times may have you experiencing grief from the death of a loved one or from divorce. Your grief may be due to the loss of your health from sickness or aging. Maybe you've lost your way, your job, your hope, you're lonely, tired, and feel like it's never going to get better—and maybe you think you don't deserve better anyway.

Throughout the book as I speak of grief or loss, the gamut runs wide; but whatever the cause, there is a common pitfall—it tries to take away our hope, thereby taking away our joy.

While writing this book I often fretted over what words to use, how to organize the pages, and what to say or what not to say. I fretted over how to present the paragraph you just read. I spent tireless months on trying to get it just right. After much lamenting, and at times thinking I was in way over my head, I finally asked myself, did I want to make a perfect book, or did I simply want to share a message of perfect hope? My answer came quickly.

I wrote this book to encourage the sad, lonely, tired, stressed, depressed, bereaved, or otherwise grieved. To share stories, words, and ideas that may help strengthen your hope—a hope that will see you through life's hurts and hardships. And not just get through the hardships, but experience joy along the way. It is my hope that you find something that resonates within your spirit, and that it helps move you beyond whatever struggles you may be going through. I've also blended together beautiful and uplifting images with soulful and spiritual quotes, scriptural verses, and other meaningful thoughts for reflection and meditation.

Additionally, I briefly discuss a topic that is an integral part of our journey in hope and joy—our thoughts. It's important to make the distinction between our feelings and our thoughts. It's okay to feel frustrated, sad or lonely. However, it's not okay to think you're unworthy, useless, undeserving, or never going to feel good again. These negative thoughts which too often accompany our feelings, will rob us of our joy. Our feelings we can embrace, it is our thoughts we must learn to restore with hope and happiness.

We grieve because we've lost someone or something of value: a life, our health, a relationship, or maybe our self-worth. We grieve because we love, because we care, and intrinsically we know there is more for our life. In order to heal and be strengthened, we must allow ourselves to feel our pain. There isn't one big thing that can be done to make it all better, nor should there be; healthy grief is a process that strengthens our heart. However, there are small things that we can do along the way that will make our burden a little less heavy and our path a little brighter. I hope the words in this book will inspire and encourage you, and that you can glean something that will help you find your way through—not to a perfect life, but to a life of perfect hope.

I was born without a right hand and forearm, so at a very early age I faced adversity, both emotional and physical. I quickly learned how to overcome self-doubt, and I found creative and often unconventional ways to move beyond the challenges I faced. In my work, I encounter many people struggling—yet overcoming—their own challenges: spousal, parental or child loss, low self-esteem, loneliness, anxiety, bi-polar disorders and depression. So it is that I share a little about what has helped them, and what has helped me, to hang on to our hope, and to find our *how*—even through the tough times. I don't know if what works for me, or what works for another, will work for you—but it might, and we offer it to you with a mighty hope that it does.

On a personal note, I've included a few journal entries I made throughout the course of my mom's illness. Mom still encourages me through these words I wrote over twenty years ago. I share them in hopes she can encourage you too. You'll also find me using anecdotes and analogies; occasionally, I will reference a teddy bear. It was a teddy bear that changed the direction of, and helped me find purpose in my life; so I kind of like them—besides, I thought it might be nice to have some gentle, sweet faces to accompany you through the pages of the book.

However, *Bear with Hope* is not about teddy bears, but about how to make small steps that help us hang on to hope and experience joy through tough times. It's about making the choice to be happy by developing an attitude that empowers us. Having a hopeful and joyful heart isn't a state we just arrive at; it is cultivated by the choices we make daily. By stringing together a whole lot of little choices that bring hope and joy, we can create a lifetime of it.

Tammy

Hope for the Heart

Hope is important because it can make the present moment less difficult to bear. If we believe that tomorrow will be better, we can bear a hardship today. —Thich Nhat Hanh

It was the day after Thanksgiving, 1996 that we laid our mama to rest. She was only fifty-five. For two years she fought the battle against that dreadful disease—breast cancer. I often heard the term "battling" cancer, and never really quite knew what that meant until I watched my mother endure the vicious assault the cancer made on her body. It eventually metastasized to her bones and over time destroyed her tailbone. It came to the point where she couldn't walk or even sit. The last eight months of her life were spent in bed.

Although her body succumbed, her mind and spirit only grew stronger. I learned a lot during this time—about her and about myself. As I witnessed my mother experience such seemingly senseless pain and agony, I questioned a lot of things—my faith, my God. Like most people, I asked w*hy? Why do bad things happen to good people?* We come to different conclusions based on our upbringing, environment, and religious or spiritual beliefs; but whatever our conclusion is, it is essential we find peace and purpose within ourselves. I came to my peace not with answering the *why*, but with finding the *how*.

We've all been hurt by life—and by death. We experience frustrations, strife, sadness, and sorrow. Life events and circumstances can cause anything from minor disappointment to major depression. Yet the same circumstances will develop wisdom and strength within us, if we allow them to. The trials and challenges that test our emotional and mental fortitude must be met with hope. Having hope is not a passive stance; we can and should be active in our search for finding and strengthening our hope. With hope, we persevere, and through perseverance, we overcome. Hope doesn't take the pain away, but it sure helps us work through the tough times.

Mama raised six girls, and I am the youngest. Those stories you hear about the baby getting all the attention? I'm here to tell you they're all true. For me, though, it seems it wasn't enough just to be the baby; I was a little different as well—I was born with only one hand. My right arm did not develop much past my elbow, leaving me with a little nub and five pea-sized fingers. At the time, the doctors couldn't tell us why it happened, or even a give us a good medical explanation, but later in life, I would give it reason; I would find its purpose.

Despite having only one hand, I've always liked to make things. I also like vintage stuff, and enjoy finding things to fix up and re-purpose. You will often find me at garage sales, antique stores, and thrift stores, looking to find that something special to give new life to.

Some time ago, I was wandering through one of my favorite stores, and as always, I was eager to sort through the orphaned teddy bears. I searched the pile of bears tossed in a big wire bin at the back of the store, hoping to find that special one to rescue. I reached for a fluffy brown one and then grabbed a little white one. I held them and wondered what their stories were. If teddy bears could talk, what would they say? I questioned what purpose each had. I imagined some were birthday or anniversary bears, perhaps some get-well bears, or my favorite, the "just-because" bears.

I looked around and noticed a woman pushing a buggy sparsely filled with odds and ends. I glanced down at the floor and couldn't help noticing her shoes. It seemed as though they had walked a few miles. I turned my attention back to the teddy bear in my hand; it looked as though it had been through those same miles. I wondered what secrets, hopes, and tears it must be filled with.

Still rummaging through the bins, I noticed an elderly gentleman walking by. His face was marked with age spots, and deep wrinkles surrounded his eyes and defined his smile. I considered what stories he must have, what pain he'd been through, and what wisdom he had gathered in his life. Likewise with the pile of teddy bears—what stories would they tell if only they could speak?

As I hold these bears, I look beyond their lifeless stuffed fur and consider the lives of the people to whom they belonged. I think about the celebrations and the pain these bears have witnessed, and the capacity for compassion a teddy bear could attain if it were real. The teddy bears look back at me; some are happy and some sad. Some are big, some small, and they come in an assortment of colors, sizes, and textures. I recognize how different they appear; yet, they are still all teddy bears—as unique and diverse as the people who once held them in their hands.

Few things in life are certain. Once born into the world, death is the only certainty we all must face. Tragically, death comes too soon for some, while others journey on, further experiencing both the joys and heartaches of life. We are much like teddy bears. We can have a life of love—or a life of use or abuse—smiles can fade, seams break, the stuffing falls out, leaving only an empty shell. With teddy bears, it's easy to throw out something tattered and torn and just buy a new one. However, with a little time and care, we could stuff, fluff, stitch it up, and restore it to new beauty and purpose.

But what about us—what do we do when life knocks the stuff out of us? What can we do when we feel empty, tattered, and torn? Instead of being dragged around by the ear or stuffed in a chest, we are broken down by the suffering and stress that comes with life. It is then that we are challenged with finding ways to pick up our stuff, add some new, and put it all back together—in hopes of being whole again.

Two years after Mama died, I saw a local television program about a company that makes teddy bears out of old fur coats. I thought of Mama's coat that I often saw hanging in the closet. Sometimes, I took a moment to touch it, to smell it, and just remember her arms wrapped around me with so much love. It was not fancy, just a well-worn, furry old coat that so many times hugged my mama in warmth.

So the idea of her coat becoming a teddy bear seemed perfect to me. I could take Mama's coat and give new life to it! I could restore it to something of beauty, something of use, a teddy bear I can wrap my arms around, touch, and embrace, and let absorb my tears. Something with a sweet, comforting face looking back at me. I knew I wanted a teddy bear.

I eagerly called to make arrangements for Mama's bear to be made, yet when I told them Mama's coat was a synthetic fur coat, they informed me their procedure was to use only "real" fur coats. Mama's coat was a plush, wooly fur; to me, it was just as real as I was sitting there. Their response ignited a fire within me, and it was all I needed to proclaim, "I'll just make it myself!"

I am not really sure why I thought that. I didn't own a sewing machine, and I couldn't sew two stitches, let alone make a teddy bear, especially with just one hand. I was good with a glue gun, but not needle and thread. Nonetheless, by that time, it didn't matter; my mind and my heart were made up. So began my journey—I was going to make a teddy bear.

As accustomed as I was doing things differently than others, somehow, some way, I thought I'd figure this bear-making out as I needed to. I jumped head—or should I say heart—first into making Mama's teddy bear. I felt challenged, but enthusiastically so. Day after day, I worked to make my bear, but day after day, I struggled, only to become increasingly discouraged. It wasn't long before my enthusiasm began to fade.

What was excitement turned to frustration. I tried to manage my new sewing machine, but it was just too difficult. I couldn't control the pedal; I would go too fast and then too slow, all the while trying to guide the thick curved parts of the fur under a sharp, very fast-moving needle. I couldn't even sew an ear.

After several attempts, discouraged and frustrated, I sadly put the idea away. There was no way I could make a teddy bear. I couldn't sew, and especially not with just one hand. I pushed the sewing machine aside, and for a while, it just sat, abandoned. I caught a glimpse of it from time to time and asked myself if I was really giving up. After all, I'd spend twenty minutes trying to put on a bracelet rather than asking for help, simply because I needed to know I could do it. But with this, it was *really* hard; I needed two hands to make a bear, not to mention a few sewing skills.

Several days later, I remembered what Mama would say, and how proud she would be. I could not give up. Mom told me I could do anything I wanted to if I believed I could. So with those words echoing in my mind—and my heart—I made my first teddy bear. Little did I know that bear would change the direction and purpose of my life.

When we cling to hope for accomplishment, happiness, and peace, or in desiring more for our life, we must also persevere beyond the circumstances and thoughts that keep us down. There were many things cluttering and clogging up my mind that tried to keep me from making Mama's bear:

- ♥ I have only one hand
- ♥ I don't know how to sew
- ♥ It would take too much time to learn
- ♥ How could I follow a pattern even if I had one
- ♥ I'm afraid to ruin Mama's coat if I cut it up
- ♥ I really don't want a teddy bear anyway (amazing what we tell ourselves when we don't want to commit to something or are fearful to step out of our comfort zone)
- ♥ I'm afraid I'll fail and be more depressed than I already am

While we experience negative thoughts, we must not let them control our belief in ourselves. Yes, I felt frustrated, sad and disappointed, all of which are natural responses to conflict and anguish. However, there is no place for faulty judgments about ourselves, such as, "I'll never be happy again," "I can't do that," or "I'm not any good..." With effort, we can learn to refuse their demand for attention.

Much of my early bear making was done sitting on the floor using my toes, my knees, my chin, and my teeth; anything to compensate for the hand I do not have. But what I did have was the belief in myself that I could do it. I wrapped thread around my toes to tie off knots. I used my knees to hold pieces together and to join the complicated parts of the teddy bear. Even with two hands, the mechanics of making a bear is challenging, but with one hand, it is even more so, and at times, it felt impossible. Yet what seemed impossible became possible.

Occasionally I will have people see my bears and say, "Wow, I wish I could sew." or "I could never do that." In return I always say, "I never would have thought I could either—until I tried."

It was a choice I was given the opportunity to make. Whether it's making a teddy bear, changing self-defeating thoughts, or finding joy in the toughest of times, it's a choice we have. Whatever it is that you are being challenged with, you can work through and beyond it. It isn't easy at times, and may take some unconventional means, but sometimes, that's just what it takes.

Someone once sent me a letter expressing to me the severe depression she lived with daily. She said getting out of bed was a huge feat, and there were many days she didn't want to live. However, she shared with me that since discovering my teddy bears and knowing I made them with only one hand, her thinking had changed, as had her belief in herself and what she could accomplish. Every morning, she looked at her bear and she would put one foot on the floor, then the other, and tell herself she can do anything—that if I could do it, so could she. She had two feet, two legs, two hands, and she *could* do it. Little does she know how often I have gleaned motivation from her.

Sometimes, it's easier giving up than investing the time and effort it takes to bring about something we desire. Hopeful, happy, joy-filled people actively practice ways to move past the obstacles that get in their way. They keep moving forward, through, around, above and beyond whatever challenge it is that tries to keep them from their goal or

purpose. We must believe in ourselves and be grateful it is a choice that we are given the opportunity to make.

Most all of us have experienced some level of sorrow or depression in our life. Whether it's been for a few minutes, a day, a few months, or years, there is a range of situations and circumstances that cause grief and sorrow. When the source is from something specific, we can usually get back to a sense of normalcy. Depending on our setback, situation, or loss, the duration of sadness may take a little longer to get through, and we learn to adjust to a new normal, but we do recover from the initial intense pain.

A feeling of sadness is okay; it's a healthy, normal response to certain situations. What is not okay is a state of depression. When we are facing difficult circumstances, we may have depressed moods for a period of time, but we recover. We accept our new normal and learn to move forward. However, major depression is a deeper, darker feeling of hopelessness and despair. Major depression can be present without a specific cause, although it often develops during difficult times.

What we want is to keep our grief from becoming major depression and for depression to be realized and appropriately addressed. If you, or someone you know, is withdrawn, using outlets such as alcohol, drugs, or other destructive behaviors, I encourage you to reach out on their behalf or on your own; there is someone who can walk with you, you need not bear your pain alone. Please seek guidance from a friend, clergy, your doctor, or another mental health professional.

The Girl with One Arm

*I*t's never easy being a teenager, and being physically different than everyone else doesn't help much either. My seventh-grade year was a very emotionally challenging and difficult one. In 1981, my mom and stepdad picked fruit and often spent the summer and fall months following the apple harvests. The frequent moves between Arkansas, Missouri, and Oklahoma were tumultuous on my school year causing me to transfer schools multiple times, and it was tough.

I had never been to a big city, and going to the city in my home town in Arkansas meant going to Russellville, population 14,000. So when I found myself at a junior high school in Oklahoma City, population over 400,000, I was petrified. I was truly a misfit and utterly out of place. I remember I was teased and often made fun of because of the clothes and shoes I wore. I was a simple, poor country girl, with a strong southern accent and became known as "the girl with one arm."

Making friends was not easy, and I was very lonely, especially during group activities or at lunchtime. I desperately wanted to hide out in the girls' restroom and would have if the school hadn't kept them locked. However, as difficult a time as I went through at this school, it provided me with an extraordinarily positive experience I will never forget.

It was movie day, so all the students gathered in the gym for the presentation of an educational film entitled *The Truly Exceptional.* The movie was meant to educate students, and help show perspective of people with disabilities. On this day, the film was about Carol Johnston, a former All-American gymnast from Cal State University.

Once the film started, I gazed upon the screen, and soon became mesmerized. Carol was just like me! In all of my thirteen years, I had never seen anyone with an arm like mine. For all I knew, I was the only one in the world. I was captivated by Carol, not only because of her one hand, but also because she excelled at gymnastics. Despite the physical challenge, gymnastics was something I had longed to do. I know how hard I tried, and then how excited I was when I did my first one-handed back walk-over. I worked incredibly hard to do something that others thought I couldn't. But I knew I could—if I just tried hard enough—and believed I could. Seeing someone like me was encouraging and inspiring, especially during a time when I felt so alone and out of place.

Carol doesn't know about me or my story, but I would love to share with her and thank her for how much she helped me. I was only at that school a short while, but my time there was long enough to learn about Carol and realize I was not alone. I am also grateful to the teachers who shared the film. I've often thought it was shown because of me. While it was the first time I saw someone like me, it was likely the first time the other students had seen someone like *me*. It's important for each of us to know we are not alone.

It is easy to feel discouraged and hopeless in times of trials and troubles. We hurt, and no one knows what we are going through; no one knows what you are experiencing. I don't, and neither does your neighbor, doctor, or pastor. They're your challenges, your pain, and your life experience. However, most people have hurt and know the pain and *strengthening* they have gone through.

It helps to bear with one another in support and love, being aware that others have overcome similar situations or circumstances. Even if you think you have no control over your own situation, you can always be in a position to help someone have hope. When you are able to help another, it is a gift that comes from your own pain. When you do this, hope overflows from you with feelings of purpose and worthiness. Carol helped me that day by sharing her story, and now I share my story and the stories of others to help comfort and inspire hope and happiness in your heart.

Having peace, experiencing joy, and being happy is something each and every one of us can have, even amidst our trials and troubles. Bad things will happen, sad days will come, but it's what we meet those times with that will determine our emotional and physical well-being.

If you can believe, all things are possible.—Mark 9:23

*D*isappointment, frustration, and sadness are all signs that we are human and are responding to situations and circumstances because we feel. It's normal, and we should embrace these feelings. Stifling our feelings or denying them will only hinder our well-being. Pent-up grief is one of the biggest barriers to our joy. To avoid these barriers we must first allow ourselves to feel the pain and embrace our feelings. Understand their place and you will have the ability to rise above and beyond them rather than be defeated by them. While it is important that we do not deny or hide these feelings, we must be ever so mindful of the thoughts that often accompany these feelings.

I can feel sad or depressed without being in despair; I can be unsuccessful at things without being a failure. I can have bad relationships and still be lovable. A child or spouse may die, but we can go on living—and be happy again. Circumstances do not define who we are, it is how we respond to those circumstances that will strengthen—or suffocate—us. Your feelings are good; the negative thoughts that tag along are not. However this is something that can be changed, we can transform doubt into hope, worry into peace, and sorrow into joy.

Joan, the mother of a murder victim, once said that when she was first told of her daughter's death, she immediately knew she had to choose. Initially, I wondered what was she choosing—she went on to say she knew she had to choose to live. Something as tragic and senseless as this could break someone, and with that, they lose their own life, not physically, but psychologically and spiritually. This grieving mother chose life, and was able to honor the spirit and life of her daughter.

Jaycee Dugard was eleven years old when she was kidnapped by a sex offender who kept her prisoner for eighteen years until she was discovered in 2008. Jaycee, in her book, *Stolen Life: A Memoir*, encourages each of us that we can endure tough situations and survive, and not just survive, but that we can be okay on the inside, too. In an interview (Sawyer, 2010) Jaycee said at first, she cried every day, but after a while, she acknowledged that she was alive, and if she was alive, there was still hope. *Still hope.* These are words coming from a young girl who was being held captive under unimaginable circumstances, and she *chose* to have hope. There is always hope.

Working through grief, overcoming setbacks, and moving beyond challenging situations begins with our thoughts. We can all acknowledge we can't change an event that has happened. But what we can do is change how we respond to it and how we act upon it. This starts with what we allow our mind to think about. No matter your challenge, you can not only get through it, but you can get through it with hope in your heart.

Our mind is often a playground for our thoughts. Sometimes our thoughts take us on dangerous rides; sometimes they ride the merry-go-round and take us for a spin. Sometimes we're on a roller coaster, other times, they passively sit and we ruminate over the why of something or that life isn't fair. Refuse the thoughts telling you that things are hopeless, or you'll never feel joy again. We are at the control center of our thoughts, and we can put an end to the dangerous games the mind sometimes wants to play. Stopping the negative thoughts is something that requires effort, and it takes practice, but you can do it.

Studies using MRIs of the brain show that each time we think negative or angry thoughts, we are triggering an increase of blood flow to the areas of the brain that are linked to depression and anger. By this surge, we are only reinforcing the very thoughts and feelings we need to let go of. The good news is, it works the same way when we think happy and positive thoughts. When we think happy thoughts, we are rejuvenating the areas of the brain associated with happiness and well-being, thus promoting the feelings and emotions we desire.

I've developed a mindful practice to promote my well-being that I liken to cardiopulmonary resuscitation (CPR). Performing CPR can give someone another chance at life by assisting their heart. This CPR is for the heart beating in our chest, but we have another Heart—the one that is at the center of our being. What do we do for it when it is hurting or slowly dying? I offer a different kind of CPR: Commitment, Perseverance, and Restoration.

Commitment

We commit to car loans, home loans, and cable services. We commit to colleges, jobs and relationships. Yet we often find it difficult to commit to ourselves. To commit to the most valuable asset we have—our Heart. When we commit to our Heart, to not only feel better, but also to be better, we claim hope, and hope brings forth an abundance of good things: peace, joy, comfort, love, and happiness.

It takes commitment to transform our thoughts and rise above and beyond challenging events. If you're stuck in a place of strife and negative thinking, this is an opportunity to commit to change. Commitment is the first mental step we can take to discover hope, and experience our joy again.

We can't choose what life sends our way; we can't always avoid the speed bumps or speed traps. These events are going to happen; some will try to take from us the intrinsic joy we are born with. But we can choose our emotional responses to these events. Instead of suffering in your struggles, you can be strengthened in them. Despite our external circumstances, our inner self can be at peace. How amazing is that?

Commit to hope and happiness, commit to changing the thoughts that keep you down and going in circles. When all else fails, when hope seems lost, understand there is always something, no matter how small, you can choose to do to move forward. Commit to being faithful to yourself.

I am responsible.
Although I may not be able to prevent
the worst from happening,
I am responsible.
For my attitude toward the inevitable
misfortunes that darken life.
Bad things do happen.
How I respond to them defines my character
and the quality of my life.
I can choose to sit in
perpetual sadness,
immobilized by the
gravity of my loss; or
I can choose to rise
from the pain
and treasure the
most precious gift
I have...Life Itself

—Walter Anderson

Perseverance

Perseverance is the "keep on keeping on" we need to stay committed. We are often confronted with things that test our commitment. These things could be arguments, rejection, financial hardship, failure, death, negative thoughts—the list is unending. Maybe you've lost a loved one and your mind is spinning around on the *why.* Perhaps you feel disappointed because you aren't where you know you'd like to be in life. You try to stay strong and motivated, but at other times you may come up short, and that's okay too. If we slip up and lose our temper, stay in bed all day, or blow our diet by eating a second box of cookies, let's not berate ourselves because of it. Accept that it happened, acknowledge your feelings and frustrations, and gently but firmly put them in their place.

We all have hopes and dreams, and things happen that get in the way of reaching them. Perseverance will keep you moving toward the prize. Whatever that may be for you—peace, joy, happiness, love, confidence, a career, good health—stay committed, and persevere. Persevering is experiencing the events and the feelings, yet moving beyond them in a positive, forward manner. Keep going beyond; keep on keeping on.

$\mathcal{R}$estoration

$\mathcal{T}$o restore is to take something old or of no value and transform it into something with purpose and new meaning. To restore our mind is when we free ourselves from the negative, self-defeating thoughts and replace them with positive, healthy thoughts. We can restore our thoughts *and* words from negative to positive.

When you feel sad, stressed, or disappointed, that's okay; it's important to allow yourself to feel. It's a vital part of acceptance and healing. It's not so much the feelings, but the negative thoughts that piggyback on our grief, the rumination of our circumstances, that will empty us of hope. We can refuse the self-defeating, hopeless thoughts that get stuck in our head—we can jump off that merry-go-round. When these thoughts arise, let them pass, let them go, and replace them with positive, constructive, hopeful thoughts.

Commit to hope, persevere through the challenges, and restore your thoughts. These actions will lighten your heart and help get you through life's valleys with a more hopeful, positive, productive outlook.

It is good to know the life-sustaining CPR for the heart; hopefully, you'll never have to use it. But try practicing CPR for your Heart; be mindful of the thoughts that keep you going in circles. A beautiful transformation takes place when you are able to do this, and after a while, it becomes a natural process, a continual flow of mental restoration. Just as the heart constantly restores our flow of healthy blood, so, too, you can restore your thoughts.

Analogous to the CPR for our physical heart, be mindful of CPR for the Heart of your soul. The heart beating in your chest requires blood flowing freely to and away from it. The two sides of the heart work together to ensure our body is receiving only what it needs to be healthy, and that it receives nothing to harm us. The veins bring in our used, oxygen-depleted blood laced with carbon dioxide waste to the right side of the heart. In turn, the heart then sends it to the lungs where the blood is infused with life-giving oxygen, and wastes are removed and expelled.

This fresh, pure blood then flows back to the left side of the heart, which pumps it back into our body to sustain life. If the veins and arteries get clogged up or burst because of fatty foods or cholesterol, sugars, nicotine, and so on, serious (if not fatal) results are likely. This leads to pain, weakness, coldness, numbness, diseases of the heart, strokes, heart attacks, and even death.

So it is with our Heart, the soul's Heart. Our thoughts are like the blood. When we allow thoughts of an unforgiving nature, bitterness, self-doubt, or other negativity to clog up our mind, this will also lead to serious consequences—unhappiness, depression, anxiety, or the death of our joy, peace, and hope. We must learn to commit and persevere, and we must have a continual restoration of our thoughts; this keeps the Heart open to a life of love and peace.

Our experiences in life will challenge our commitment; whether it's circumstances from within or circumstances from without. When faced with challenging situations that cause negative, self-defeating thoughts and behaviors, remember your commitment, push through with perseverance, and restore your mind with positive, constructive, and hopeful thoughts—and you will find peace and experience joy.

We can transform our thoughts; it is a process that isn't always easy—but it is a process that always works.

- ♥ Commitment—I pledge to myself that I will live with hope, that I will actively practice ways to pursue happiness and experience joy in life. I understand, and am grateful that this is my choice to make.
- ♥ Perseverance—I refuse to allow thoughts, situations, circumstances, or others to get in the way of my commitment.
- ♥ Restoration—When I think thoughts like "I'll never be happy" or "I can't…" or "Life isn't fair, why me?" I will restore my thoughts with positive affirmations such as: "Not only will I be happy, I am happy… Circumstances do not define me" or "I have much to be grateful for" and "I can, I will, I am…" and "I choose hope."

We also restore our thoughts with positive actions. The remaining pages of this book offer suggestions, ideas, personal stories, and simple, effective ways to restore your thoughts—and to restore your hope.

Thursday, December 14, 1995

I didn't get to see Mom today. I've been trying not to think about losing her, it hurts too much. I really don't want to think about it. But I know it's there. She has some good days and it gives us hope, but then her pain is unbearable at times, and she is so strong to deal with it. I can tell it's a constant fight to try and feel good. But she chooses to anyway. She could easily just lie around and pity herself, but she doesn't. She gets up, dresses, and still wants to clean her house and do things. She fights everyday to do these things, even with a smile on her face. Many people and probably me—in her pain would just take as much pain medication as we could, but not Mama, she doesn't want to just lay around half out of her wit. She wants to be present, and that even means present with her pain.

Discovering Hope

With Hands and Heart
Creativity
For the Spirit
Prayer and Meditation
Giving and Gratitude
Words and Laughter
Soul Medicine
Music and Nature
Touching Hope

Hope in Creativity

God has given each of you some special abilities; be sure to use them to help each other, passing on to others God's many kinds of blessings.—1 Peter 4:10

Implementing creative arts in our life is a meaningful, yet simple way to discover hope and experience joy. The creative process elevates our mood, increases blood flow, and boosts our immune system. It promotes the release of our happiness hormones and helps to quash the stress-causing ones. Enjoying music, painting, poetry, writing, sewing, or any other activity that encourages mental or physical involvement can also offer much-needed distraction from any sorrow or stress you are going through.

Creative channels such as these are both relaxing and rewarding and can be a positive way to help experience joy and feel peace in otherwise challenging times. Simply turning a blank canvas or sheet of paper into something with shapes and forms, color and contrast, is an incredible source of fulfillment and delight. Capturing a moment in time with the lens of a camera or shaping big clumps of clay in to something of beauty and purpose keeps us in touch with our senses, and in harmony with the present. The ability to create is in all of us; it's a matter of listening to our Heart and allowing ourselves to experience it.

Self-expression through art is a well-known practice proven valuable; art stimulates areas of our brain that helps promote positive emotions and well-being. While art therapy is beneficial, so, too, is creative art we can do on our own, and all we need are a few inexpensive supplies and a willing and open Heart.

A pencil and paper, paintbrush and canvas, or colored pencils and coloring book are enough to help release your creativity. My stepdad is seventy-seven years old and has recently taken up drawing in adult coloring books. From flowers and fairies to geometric designs and mandalas, the pages are just waiting to be filled in with color. He says coloring is not only time for him to relax and enjoy, but creating something beautiful gives him a feeling of accomplishment. Both viewing and creating art helps increase levels of dopamine in our brain, and this in turn just simply makes us feel better and provides a sense of purpose and well-being.

From Darkness to Light

A few years ago I was going through a debilitating depression. I felt as if everything in my life was falling apart. I suffered tremendous loss and reached a point in my life I wanted it to be over. Therapy and medication helped at times, but I needed more. I needed something to touch me deeper. One day a friend invited me to an art class just for fun, I didn't need any paint supplies, or even skills, they provided it all, well maybe not the skill, but the supplies. But it was just to be for fun, so why not? At first I was hesitant and robotically applied paint to the canvas, but as time went on, and with each stroke I felt something unwinding. I began to relax and without reservation or hesitation let the brush flow all over the place. I felt a glimmer of hope. There was something freeing about letting loose my emotions and allowing my feelings to flow through the paint. I was hooked and started painting on my own. I acquired my own painting supplies, not worried about the painting skills I didn't have, because I had my emotions. It wasn't about being a good painter; it was about being able to let myself express my feelings and emotions. At first, the colors were drab and dark, but as I allowed my pain to be filtered through the paint, the canvas became brighter, more vibrant, and so did my life.—Tina

Turn on your favorite music and sketch or paint the trees, daisies or dandelions out in your backyard. Sign up for an art class, or invite someone to one. A simple invitation to someone hurting can change their life, or yours. We never know when, or where, we will find that flicker, that glimmer of hope. Expressing ourselves through creativity provides a constructive outlet for our feelings, and triggers our brain to release the endorphins similar to that of antidepressants; how much more fun and rewarding to experience it with a pencil or paintbrush! Painting, sculpting, photography, drawing, they afford moments of reprieve from feeling sadness or stress. It's building on these moments that will see you through each day. Before you are fully aware of the change, the anxieties or sorrow you feel will begin to lift their weight from you and expose the colors of life, joy, and hope.

I find hope in the darkest of days, and focus in the brightest. I do not judge the universe.—Dalai Lama XIV

The Sunrise

My story is one of tragedy followed by good fortune. It is the story of death giving birth to life and of the power of photography to make it happen.

I had always considered myself a common man living a common life. Being the head of a business consulting firm provided me with little time to pursue some of my interests aside from work. I was concentrated on growing my company and making a name in the industry.

However, I would eventually come to learn that life is always unpredictable and that it only takes a split second for things to change forever. In December of 2009 my wife was diagnosed with cancer and suddenly all my time and effort were being redirected toward fighting a four-year long battle, which we sadly lost. She passed away in April of 2013 leaving me behind after ten years together.

My wife may have died physically but in many ways, I died along with her. There are just no words to describe the pain and loneliness that I felt. I was lost and crippled. For several months I struggled to perform even the simplest of daily activities and I could hardly find a reason to enjoy life again. I was cruising through a storm and in desperate need of a safe harbor.

Then, one morning, I woke up to an epic sunrise. Living in South Florida I was used to them but this one was special. I went out to the balcony and felt a strong presence of my wife in that amazing scene. I snapped a picture with my phone and decided to share it with my friends on social media. The next day I was compelled to do the same. Soon after, I was capturing every sunrise and posting them on social media. People's reactions were surprising and their positive comments lifted my spirit.

A friend of mine suggested that I take my interest more seriously so at thirty-nine years of age I bought my first semi-pro DSLR and took a couple of lessons with a local photographer to learn the basics.

I will never forget the very first time I pressed the shutter of my camera. Not because of the stunning sunrise that I was able to capture (beginner's luck) but rather because of the unexpected effect it had on me. That press of the button ignited a flame in my heart. A flame, which quickly became a wildfire that roared inside my soul.

Photography not only became a much-needed distraction but it also helped me to express my feelings and my pain in a way that I felt comfortable with. At first, the subjects I decided to shoot and the titles I used for my images reflected the darkness that wandered in my life but gradually my pictures started to show some hints of light and hope, a clear sign that my recovery was in process.

I became obsessed and addicted to photography. My entire time was devoted to studying and learning as much as I could. For months I read every single book and magazine I could put my hands on and practiced daily whatever new technique I came across. As any photographer would attest, the camera teaches you to see your surroundings with new eyes and a new mindset. Not only did I start to appreciate many things that I had taken for granted but I also began to notice the beauty that had always been there but somehow I had been blind to. Raindrops on a leaf, the reflection of clouds on the ocean, the subtle shades of green in a tree.

I started traveling to National Parks all across the US and abroad, spending countless days by myself, hiking, camping and photographing. Soon I experienced the mysterious ways that nature has to heal hurting souls. And while exploring in solitude the stunning and vast wilderness I also probe deep into my soul. With every click of my camera shutter, I started to recognize a new self. One who understood the meaning of life a little better than before.

For my fortieth birthday, I decided to make a solo trip to Arches National Park, Utah. That November 20, 2013, while shooting the sunrise at around 5:30 am, I was fortunate enough to experience a once-in-a-lifetime moment: complete and utter silence. In the middle of the desert, absent of even the slightest sound of civilization or nature, I was finally able to listen to my heart and decided to follow my passion for photography in a more serious and professional manner.

Landscapes are my specialty although I also enjoy wildlife and natural abstracts. The Atlantic Ocean is my backyard so seascapes are a frequent subject; however, I am especially drawn to the mysticism and energy of the desert. The American Southwest is one of my favorite places to shoot.

I have no other goal than to add value to people's lives by sharing images from the most beautiful and bizarre places around the world. To elicit strong emotions in those who view my photographs. To make them feel as if they are standing right there beside me. However, it is often said that photography should serve a higher purpose. If so, I wish to motivate people to go out and explore the natural world as I did. To connect with it in their own special way and to protect it, for our sake and that of future generations.

I hope my story proves that it is never too late to find and pursue a passion. I also hope that it serves as an example of how life, while unpredictable and sometimes fierce, can always provide a second chance or, as I like to call it, a new sunrise.—Fernando

Other creative approaches that might prove hopeful, helpful, and fun are crafting, sewing, cooking, reading, writing and creative exercise. These are all simple and effective ways to build emotional strength and purpose. Many of these activities help re-direct our mind on a goal, we create something beautiful, and while we enjoy it ourselves, we can share it with others. Experiment with different activities, keep your heart open and you may very well find a flicker of hope in a newfound joy.

The best way to cheer yourself up is to try to cheer somebody else up.—Mark Twain

ittle Dresses for Africa is an organization with a wonderful group of people who make little dresses for children in Africa. Sweet and simple dresses are made out of pillowcases and given to the orphanages, churches, and schools in Africa. It is their hope to instill the belief in each of the girls that they matter. Their belief is: *"We're not just sending dresses, we're sending hope."*

Little Dresses for Africa is based out of Michigan, but they have volunteers in all fifty states and welcome pillowcase dresses from hearts and hands across the country.

I never knew how to run a sewing machine until I made my first bear, but I was always good with a glue gun. If I had silk flowers, lace, ribbon, and a glue gun, I could make some pretty crafty things. If you are crafty, or even if you're not, it's easy to pick up some materials from the craft store and make some flower arrangements or a wall wreath. Crafting is a creative and fun way to spend time refocusing the mind, restoring your thoughts, and it will also turn out something you can share. Consider gifting a flower arrangement to residents at your area nursing home, women's shelter or local ministry that serves those less fortunate.

At the age of sixteen, I began working as an aide at a nursing home. The three years I spent growing up there made a significant impact on my life. The loneliness, rejection, and sadness I witnessed with many of the residents is almost too hard for the heart to experience. Some residents are alone and have no family and no comforts of home. A small flower arrangement might just make their day...along with a teddy bear.

If you want others to be happy, practice compassion.

If you want to be happy, practice compassion

—Dalai Lhama

Skye Rose Bears

Faith Unseen

My story isn't about discovering hope with anything creative that I do or have done...but with what someone else created. About 5 years ago I was diagnosed with multiple sclerosis. I had recently lost my husband to a devastating illness, had to change careers to support myself, and my teenage son began acting out. It was a very hard time.

Then one day I began feeling a little disoriented. Within a week I couldn't walk, and I had limited movement in my arms. I was hospitalized long term. I thought I could not take anymore and maybe I should just let go and die—everything was just too much. I wasn't sure what I had to live for. Somehow I was able to make it through rehab and was slowly recovering, but I still felt overwhelmed with what my next step was.

I was very lonely, so I decided to find a rescue dog to save, really to save us both. While searching online I came across some clay sculptures of little puppies and cats, bears and rabbits. These were the cutest things I had ever seen. The sweet faces on these clay pieces just brought joy to my heart. It was then I read the about the artist only to discover she was blind. She was blind! I was beyond amazed, I was amazed just when I knew someone had actually made these by hand, but blind? I have since returned to work full-time, and my son and I have re-connected. And, yes, I did find a dog to adopt, who is now my closest companion. This artist truly touched me,
and has been my inspiration. When I am feeling down or discouraged, I look at her art. So although I have yet to find a creative spark in me, I found it in someone else, and I thank her for sharing her art and her heart with the world. —Celia

Balancing Beads

I have bi-polar disorder. I've dealt with it since late adolescence. It has affected my goals, my dreams and my hopes. I was given medication—a bunch of medication. After a few months, I would quit taking it because the side effects were horrible. I gained fifty pounds and had no interest in anything. Although while off my medication I would have these incredible days, even weeks of just being so happy and having all the fun in the world, I'd stay up nights with all the new and exciting things I wanted to do. Then out from nowhere I'd wake up and wish I would never wake up again. I hurt, my heart was heavy, and I felt sick and disgusted. Disgusted with myself, my body, my mind, my life, and the world. However, I detested taking the medication, it made me fat, and often lethargic. While it helped stabilize my moods, it also took away my joy. My counselor suggested I take up a hobby, so I started making jewelry, or more specific, beading. At first I thought it was too tedious, how could it help me? And besides it was time-consuming, but then, what was I doing with my time anyway? My doctor agreed to lower my medication dose to one that wouldn't completely sedate me, and I learned to bead as part of my therapy. I beaded when I felt depressed, it gave me a sense of accomplishment, and it gave me purpose. I beaded if I felt a manic state sneaking up, it gave me a sense of calmness and clarity. I made my necklaces using mostly tiny seed beads, so it required much focus and attention. Without beading, I really had no purpose to focus, it wasn't that I couldn't, I just didn't have a need to.

I found myself creating more and more, not out of mania, or depression, but out of joy. I gave them as gifts and soon began selling my jewelry, and even getting custom requests. I am now on a minimum

Three O'Clock Bears

dosage of a new medication, this allows me to still be me, but provides a base level of stabilization, but beading remains my main mode of therapy. Beading helped me focus, it gave me purpose, and provided an outlet for what once was my weakness, to what is now my strength.—Lea

Lea found meaning and purpose in making beautiful things. It helped to find balance in her life. This activity not only helped her, but gave joy to others—what woman doesn't love to wear beautiful jewelry, especially a one-of-a-kind piece!

Lea takes tiny beads and makes jewelry to wear, I like to take bits of fabric and materials and create something to touch; other people can take flour, sugar, and raw eggs and create something delicious for our taste and tummy. I remember as a child I would smell vanilla extract, and how heavenly it smelled, but as soon as I tasted it, yuck! Vanilla by itself is awful to taste, but unite it with other ingredients and how delightful it becomes to taste as well. When individual ingredients come together, they can make a delicious finished result. It's the same for our emotional health; it takes a lot of little things put together to get the result we desire—happiness and emotional well-being.

Writing and Journaling

Journaling, poetry, keeping a diary or creative writing is a form of self-expression that allows us the chance to release inner fears, frustrations, hopes, or dreams. By no means have I ever considered myself a writer, yet here I sit. It's not so much about great writing skills, but about self-expression, and for me, sharing a message. You will be joyfully surprised what is inside if you choose to listen.

The longest duration I've ever kept a journal was throughout the first year of Mama's illness. I'm ever so thankful for those written memories from over twenty years ago. Moments in time with Mom I would have forgotten. Memories of her fight, but more importantly memories of her strength, humor, and faith.

We don't need to write a novel or compose a symphony—just write our feelings. Write a memory you have. Write about a time in your life that you experienced joy. Write about a sad time and how you made it through. Writing gives you an inner release of fear and frustrations, or it can be a way of positively expressing your hopes and dreams, and can give you time to recapture a joyful experience.

Reading

Getting lost in a book is an incredible way to give us freedom from worry; a temporary escape from the woes of life. Take a journey into a different time and place with a good novel, or better yet, grow your knowledge of different cultures, places, and people.

What do you find fascinating? The stars in the universe or amazing ocean life? The history of guitars, golf, or gardening? There are no limits to what the mind can learn, and the time you spend reading will not only improve your knowledge but give you something positive and productive to spend your thoughts on.

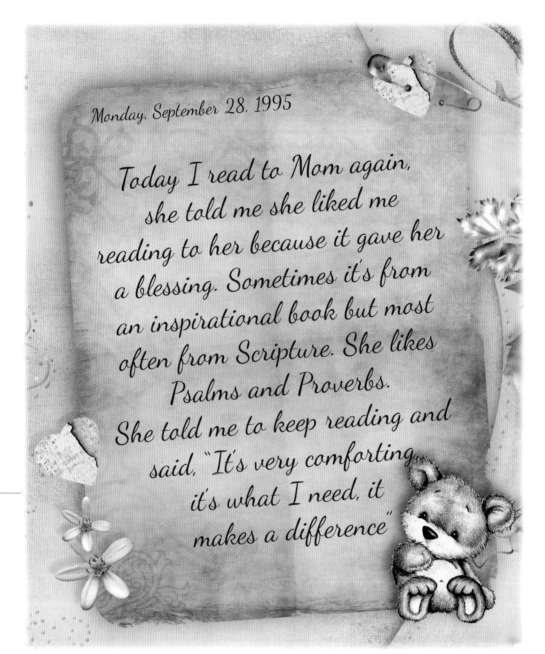

Monday, September 28, 1995

Today I read to Mom again,
she told me she liked me
reading to her because it gave her
a blessing. Sometimes it's from
an inspirational book but most
often from Scripture. She likes
Psalms and Proverbs.
She told me to keep reading and
said, "It's very comforting,
it's what I need, it
makes a difference"

Monday, September 11, 1995

I'm with Mom right now. She's resting. I'm so tired. I cried a lot last night. Cried and cried. I was afraid I wouldn't be able to stop. I just wanted it to be a bad dream. I just want to wake up and all of Mama's pain just be gone. Mom called me last night, she was really hurting. She was crying. Her cough was worse and she has a new pain near her lungs. I don't know how she

does it. She's so strong. I read to her earlier, from Psalms and from the little blue book. She really enjoys me reading to her. I rubbed her tummy, she said she was feeling sick. I laid down beside her on the bed and fell asleep a few minutes. I could have slept forever right there with Mom. She even covered me up like when I was little. My stomach had been aching, but I could only think of how insignificant my pain was compared to Mom's. I didn't want to get up.

Mom wasn't able to sit up and read herself, but having someone read to her was something she needed for her spirit, something that lifted her above the pain. One of Mom's favorite verses was:

At least there is hope for a tree: If it is cut down, it will sprout again, and its new shoots will not fail. Its roots may grow old in the ground and its stump die in the soil, yet at the scent of water it will bud and put forth shoots like a plant.—Job 14:7–10

While collecting personal stories for *Bear with Hope*, I looked for individuals who recognized their struggles, and who pushed through to the other side. People who claimed healing and hope through a variety of personal, spiritual, and creative approaches. I asked one woman to share about the value of her garden, but I could just have easily asked her to share about her painting, reading or poetry. I was mindful of the deep personal losses she has experienced and knew she utilized creative avenues for self-expression and for pushing through the tough times. Her personal story is a beautiful and meaningful example of using creative outlets while earnestly seeking hope and healing.

To Run With Wolves

I was cracking open. I didn't know what to think or do with myself. I didn't know what was real anymore. I didn't know who or what to trust— all that I perceived as true and real, was not. I didn't recognize myself anymore. My dad was imprisoned for life for pedophilia, and my son a heroin addict—imposing his own life sentence. I failed as a mom. I was a daughter of a pedophile. I spiraled into darkness. I was numb and could not begin to deal with all the negative feelings and things happening. And I didn't. I abandoned my family. I abandoned the God I knew. I abandoned myself. I could not pray. I couldn't comprehend a god that would allow this. I was obsessed with why all this was happening.

My marriage also suffered. My husband knew how much I was struggling and contacted a therapist that specialized in civilian PTSD. When I went to see her, she asked what I hoped to accomplish in therapy. I said, "a new perspective". To begin my new therapy, I started to write. Poetry soon began to flow out of my soul. It was like a pressure release valve! The words on paper helped me purge emotion I could not otherwise let out. The poetry was cathartic. It seemed natural. I couldn't understand how beauty could come from such darkness, but it did, and it was truly magical.

Poetry then led me to reading more books. I soon discovered, Women Who Run with the Wolves by Clarissa Pinkola Estés. This book opened places in me that were so hidden. I found a strength and confidence that amazed me. I am now determined to learn to express my emotions, not only by feeling them, but seeing them. Until this point, I had been so out of touch with my inner truth, I didn't know it was possible to express my heart with art. I do nails for a living, so I was familiar with the feel of liquid in a paintbrush; and now something ignited in me the idea of learning to paint.

I bought a paint set and watercolor paper then began painting pictures of the spiritual connection I had discovered through Women Who Run with the Wolves. It was an amazing release of emotion! I was getting in touch with my authentic self through art. I didn't know I could even do this—my heart on paper. This felt like my child, it was creation from my soul. I gave birth to a way of dealing with and departing from the anguish and sorrow I was feeling. The disconnecting with the anguish was the beginning of reconnecting with a place I call my higher self.

All the while I was learning to cope with my grief; my son was slipping away. Even I didn't realize how immersed he was into darkness. Heroin addiction was taking his life. I was helpless, yet could only stand by and watch. It was like watching my baby toddle on the edge of a cliff, and I am chained to a tree unable to save him. He could fall to his death at anytime and I was truly helpless.

I painted pictures from my most primal state. Then I painted a chrysanthemum, it was a totem that meant hope. I was purging. Art saved me. I dove into my soul and pulled everything out. I knew how to do this. I knew it would get emotions out of me that could damage my heart. Although I felt helpless to see my son suffer by the choices he made, I was not hopeless. Our son eventually came to a place where he was able to reach out for help, and we were there waiting.

After successfully completing rehab our son was back home. He was better and getting better every day. I dedicated my heart and soul through my art to his healing. Understanding he needed positive ways to express himself, he dug deep into his own soul through gardening. He taught himself everything he needed to know about organic gardening. He moved the earth. Watching him gave me hope. He moved the heavenly realms as far as I was concerned. I could see him healing from the inside and through the connection he had discovered with Mother Earth. The plants grew. He grew. He had hope. I had more hope. We ate the vegetables he grew. We connected in the garden.

Throughout the time our son was battling his addiction—my rock, my mom, was diagnosed with triple negative, stage 4, breast cancer. The tables were turning again. I needed to be her rock now. I painted. She took care of me all my life and now I was to take care of her. After fighting through chemotherapy and radiation, Mom went into remission and we rejoiced. But remission was short-lived; the cancer came back with a vengeance. However this time I had a newfound strength and confidence and was determined to be strong for her. I also kept painting. Her condition deteriorated and it was all physically and emotionally exhausting. She was scared and mad as hell. I held her hand. She fought. I fought beside her. Despite the turmoil, our love was all-encompassing. She lost her battle on April 12, 2016.

I knew there was only one thing I had to have of Mom's; it was the flower seeds she saved every year. I planted those precious babies, and grew a garden of my own, and watched it grow. I connected with her there. I felt her, and she sent white butterflies and dragonflies letting me know she was with me. Now our garden is filled with hope, wisdom, love and peace, it is filled with my mom. It was enough. She loved to "plant words of hope" in the lives of people she met and loved. That was her garden, a garden of hope. And it was growing. Our son was healing. I was coping, I was whole. Her seeds are being cultivated. All the brokenness was mending itself. It's as if Creation knew all along I was  going to need to purge the weeds from my soul to make room for the seeds she planted in me to grow and propagate into more and more beauty. Creating saved me—creation in poetry, painting and gardening—God is Creation to me. The evidence is in the garden of my soul, the hope which Mom planted, my art, my heart, my written words. Grief doesn't stand a chance with these weapons.—Sherri

Choose Hope

One evening, my girlfriend and I decided we were going to see what all the fuss was all about. I don't know why we thought it would be just once, soon the needle was in my arm, and three seconds later, my life changed forever. That moment would lead to so much torment, sorrow, regret, and shame. I lost whatever sense of youthful innocence I had before, and in its place grew a monster.

The next few months I went downhill very quickly. I moved back with my parents, got caught using, moved out, and broke up with the girl I loved so much. I spiraled out of control. The addiction consumed who I was. I began using all kinds of substances and became very reckless and suicidal. I had always dealt with some depression but it became immeasurably amplified. I withdrew from everyone that cared about me and resigned to a life of isolation. Alone in a disgusting cold apartment with no food and nothing to do but use and sleep when I could. I lost a bunch of weight and my skin turned a pale gray color. I wore long sleeves to cover up my arms.

Eventually, I came to a point where I couldn't go on any longer with the way things were. I had two options; end my life or try to get help. I chose to get help. I called my mom at five in the morning after a day of being up all night sick. I really needed to talk. I told her I was ready to get help, and with that, she took me to detox. During this time, she searched tirelessly until she found a place for me to go to get treatment.

Through all of this, my mom remained supportive, but she never enabled my behavior. I don't know how my parents did it, but they managed to remain in that sweet spot between support and enablement. Eventually, we found a place in a methadone clinic. This allowed me to work on myself without getting sick (mentally or physically). When I settled into the clinic I began to explore healthy creative outlets for my anxiety and depression. I began using photography, it appealed to me as a craft and a creative way for me to channel my energy. The skill involved to create something so complex yet as simple as a photograph fascinates me. The optics, the aperture, the mechanics, the emulsions, the sensors—all these things come together to capture that fleeting moment in time and space.

To anyone struggling with addiction, know that you can change yourself. To do this you must take a chance and make yourself vulnerable. You must allow others to help you and you must believe that you deserve this help. — Justin

Justin is Sherri's son. He is now twenty-four, and in recovery for over two years; he continues to practice creative means of self-expression through photography, and spends time growing and nurturing a small garden. He exercises simple ways to experience beauty and center on personal growth.

He implores parents of children who struggle with addiction to not give up hope. There's always hope; hang to it as tightly as you can. Along with parents who never gave up hope for their son, Justin believed in himself, and he is the one who ultimately made the choice to ask for help, and because of that choice, Justin has a full life ahead of him, one filled with promise and hope.

The Path

I've never been one to exercise. I even have to think twice how to spell it; sounds like it should have a Z instead of an S. Nonetheless, I know the value of exercise, both for physical and mental health well-being.

A few years ago, my husband Marc and I decided it was time for us to find an exercise that we could do together. Marc had always enjoyed bike riding, so we bought a couple of bikes and gave it a spin. He fitted my bike with an apparatus that my little right arm could fit in, which allowed for better control so that I could feel more confident and secure in handling the bike. We rode around the neighborhood for a couple of weeks before moving on to some local trails. I was energized with this new hobby. I loved it. It was a lot of fun, and it actually is exercise!

The trails were mostly gentle and quiet; they wound through wooded areas which made it all the more meaningful. I didn't even consider it exercise at all...it was too much fun. So this one beautiful evening we were going through an area of the trail that dipped down and then steeply rose back up. I had traversed it many times, but this time, I approached the incline too fast and I lost control. I went flying over the bike and my body slammed to the ground. The impact severely shattered my collarbone and subsequently shattered my bike riding career.

So now, have I encouraged you to take up trail bike riding yet? Yes, I was a little careless; I advise against that, but finding something to enjoy is what is important. It matters not what level of activity it is, explore your interests find something fun, and it will do the heart good.

Exercise provides many benefits, not just for our physical health, but our mental health. It releases endorphins that promote happiness and euphoria. Studies show a regular exercise program helps alleviate symptoms of the clinically depressed. Understanding it's hard to be motivated to exercise when often just getting out of bed or going to work is a challenge, but this is when we make the choice to rise above those thoughts and feelings that discourage us. We must fight the feelings of helplessness or hopelessness and push through and beyond the negative habits we create when we are unhappy.

An exercise activity doesn't need to be demanding or even strenuous to achieve the emotional rewards it can provide—it can be vigorous or it can be fun and relaxing. Try walking, yoga, swimming, belly dancing, or something as simple as doing the twist or jumping jacks. Throw a flying disc or a basketball. Learn to juggle or try hula dancing or hooping. Play horseshoes or badminton. Think outside the box. Whatever you commit to, it will help you experience positive emotions and feelings.

Start slow, and be realistic with what you do. Even try an exercise or activity for as little as two minutes. Studies show that creating a diversion for as little as two minutes when we are stressed or feeling down can provide just enough of a distraction we need to help build emotional strength. It's a starting place; from there, you can choose how much you allow it to help you physically and more importantly, emotionally.

It was during the time my collarbone was healing that the opportunity arose for me to write this book. I was confined to the recliner for nearly two weeks, awaiting surgery, and then another several weeks to recover. I had nothing but time on my hands—hand.

Writing a book had sparked my interest a year prior to my bike accident when asked to contribute to Mary O'Connor's book *Life is Full of Sweet Spots: An Exploration of Joy.* Mary had contacted me to share a message about the meaning of touch, and how touching teddy bears evokes a sense of joy. While sharing my stories, it resonated with my spirit. At the same time, a dear friend of mine, Bob Willis, had recently published *The Ultimate Caregiver.* I met Bob while Mom was receiving hospice care, at the time he was the bereavement coordinator and guided a grief recovery group I attended. He continues to touch the lives of people with his book, and by sharing his own creative gift of clay sculpting. I thank Mary and Bob for the spark, and I thank the bike trail for getting in my way. The path that broke my collarbone was also the path that led me to *Bear with Hope.*

Reach for the Heavens

I was once young, fit, and full of life, but as I reached my forties I quit taking care of myself, I just didn't seem to care. I was depressed, my life was going nowhere, and I had gained a lot of weight. That in turn depressed me more. It was a vicious cycle I couldn't break out of. I rarely got out in public if I didn't have to.

One day, a friend invited me to join her at a belly dancing class; she had received two free sessions. Me? Belly dancing? My belly danced every time I moved, it didn't need a class! But she insisted and said lots of full-figured women belly danced and she assured me we'd have a good time. She knew I had become a recluse and had really been struggling emotionally. After much persuasion, I relented.

Hesitant at first, regretting ever stepping out of the house, but I forced myself forward. My friend extended a hand to hold and I knew I had to do something. When I got there, I was relieved to see nobody was wearing those risqué little outfits, it was just a bunch of normal women, much like me, wearing sweats and t-shirts. Initially reserved, but when I saw others smiling and having fun I allowed myself to just relax and just be me. The first time in years I did something for just me that allowed me to have fun. I danced, and wiggled, and giggled, and my belly jiggled—and it was the most liberating experience I'd ever had. It filled me full of joy. Just being able to let go and feel free... I raised my arms and swayed and let all my negative self-talk and fearful worries out. I didn't think I could ever do something like that. I'm so grateful my friend gave me the opportunity.

When I got home, I cried. I realized how much I had been hurting myself even more by not letting go of past hurts. I was just in a cycle of grief. Dancing helped break that cycle. Sure, I still struggle with issues, but it's no longer a cycle of pain. It's been broken, and I've let hope and joy penetrate my grief.

Now I dance every day; whether I'm in a class or not, I dance. At home in the morning or in the evening, I'll turn some beautiful music on, close my eyes, raise my arms, and just sway and move like I'm reaching for the heavens and then relax my arms and let them fall to my sides. I'll spin around and sway like I'm floating in the air, but it's really my spirit that's floating. It's a very spiritual experience for me. Dancing has helped me find peace, it's helped build my self-esteem, and it's helped me connect spiritually to myself, and God. I feel free.—Cindy

Bear patiently, my heart, for you have suffered heavier things.—Homer

Tattered in to Hope

As one can imagine losing a child is such a painful event that has such an effect on every aspect of your life. Devon was twelve years old and was spending the night at her best friend's house, something she had done many times before. Only this time was different as she never returned home. She, along with her best friend and her best friend's little sister all died that night when the house caught fire.

The first few years (it's been 2009) are a blur. I remember being in shock for quite a while and feeling numb and full of despair. Not wanting to live really, the only thing keeping me going was my other two children. I'm thankful that I had wonderful friends that surrounded us right away and didn't leave our side for pretty much that whole first year

Even shopping seemed a daunting task. I would go in the middle of the night so I wouldn't have to face anyone. Getting back to our routine seemed to be a good thing. For me, though, my saving grace was my children and my husband. Our love kept us together. There isn't a day that goes by that I don't think of Devon or what happened.

For me, I had all of this extra energy—grief energy I call it. I started running every day and that seemed to help.

Every birthday, holiday, special occasion you're always reminded that someone is missing. It still pains me, but I have great faith and know that she is not really gone, just moved on, with other family that have gone before us, and are waiting for us when it is our time.

Devon had a blankey that she had from the time she was a baby. It was so worn that the silk trim had long been gone, and really it was a rag as it had been washed so many times. She slept with it every night. We were constantly on her to throw it away. That night she left it home, for that I am thankful. It was a very special piece that I had left of her and we turned that tattered scrap of a blanket into a beautiful memory bear—Wendy

Devon's Bear

I can *try* to imagine what it would be like to lose a child, but I can't wrap my mind around the depth of the pain. Wendy started running to help her expend this "grief energy" as she referred to it. Exercise can be used as a valuable productive way to release this energy. If you aren't a runner, try walking, dancing, yoga, or any other form of physical activity to help you release your own grief energy.

Wendy also had family and friends that helped get her through the darkest days, but sometimes, we don't have that, or we have family members who don't know how to deal with the difficulties themselves. This is the time when it's imperative we reach out to others who have been there or are going through similar situations.

There are supportive resources available to all of us, no matter our situation; support groups, individual therapy, pastoral care, and counseling to name only a few. If you're feeling all alone, there are resources that can help, reach out and take time to tend to the emotional and spiritual needs that will help you through the tough times.

Open to Hope is an online resource that helps people find hope after a loss. Their vision and website statement is:

> *"To provide an online forum to support people who have experienced loss: To help them cope with their pain, heal their grief and invest in their future. Open to Hope is an online website where people can share inspirational stories of loss and love. We encourage our visitors to read, listen and share their stories of hope and compassion."*

Hope makes my heart rest easy. It gives me peace amidst my struggles and sorrow. *BwH*

$\mathcal{W}$hat you leave behind is not what is
engraved in stone monuments, but what is
woven into the lives of others.—Pericles *(495-429 BCE)*

Yes, my soul,
find rest in God;
my hope comes from Him.
Psalms62:5

Prayer

We also rejoice in our sufferings, because we know that suffering produces perseverance; perseverance, character; and character, hope. And hope does not disappoint us, because God has poured out his love into our hearts by the Holy Spirit, whom he has given us.—Romans 5:3-5

rayer is a safe place to open up our heart, and allow God to fill it with His presence. It provides a place to go spiritually and emotionally; it offers hope, peace, love, and acceptance. Having a faith that is beyond our understanding can help us through our journey.

And his disciples asked him, "Rabbi, who sinned, this man or his parents that he was born blind? Jesus answered, "Neither this man nor his parents have sinned, but this happened so that the works of God might be displayed in him."—John 9:3

I've held close to my heart the preceding scripture. Throughout my life I have held to it for understanding a purpose for being born with one hand, but I also apply it to many of the struggles and challenges I encounter. Everything we consider a deficit, or heartache, every situation, event or circumstance, good or bad, are opportunities for God's power, love, and mercy to be manifested through us.

Like many, I've prayed, and prayed a lot. I've prayed to have peace, or to feel love. I pray for strength, wisdom, and joy. I can say now, I don't pray for these things in the same manner I used to. I can lose things, things are stolen, or things can be taken from me. Have you had people in your life try to steal your joy? Or circumstances rob you of it? I have, therefore by having things, we are at risk of losing them.

Biblical scripture tells us that God *is* love (1 John 4:8). I presume if you *are* something, you can't lose it and no one can steal it. I can share it and still have it fully in me. I liked this concept. So then I began applying it in my heart with not just regards to love, but also strength, peace and joy. I not only want to *have* love, I want to *be* love. I want to have joy, but I'd much rather *be* joy—just as I desire to be hope. As God perfectly embodies all of these attributes, I pray that I am more like Him. I want to have joy, but more so, I want to be joy, if I am joy that means it's there for me and for you and it never goes away. I can't lose it and no one can take it from me.

Therefore I tell you, whatever you ask in prayer, believe that you have received it, and it will be yours.—Mark 11:22-24

I have a long way to go—say a lifetime; since I still have thoughts I shouldn't, and say or do things I shouldn't, I feel I have yet to personify joy, hope or love. However, it is something I actively seek daily, through prayer and practice. Sometimes I feel it fully by His grace; other times I allow barriers—thoughts, circumstances, negative people—to get in the way and I don't feel it, think it, nor experience it like God wants me to. But I still know it's there when I choose to re-claim it—because it just *is*.

Grief: A Mother's Journey

Grief is something every human being faces at some time during their life. But all grief is not same. I have suffered grief over the loss of my parents, two sisters, a brother and dear friends, but nothing compares to the grief of losing my child. Only a parent who has lost a child can understand the unbearable, relentless sorrow. There is a unique bond between a parent and child. It is not only emotional, but somehow physical. A parent can never be separated from their child.

I lost my oldest son, Chris at the age of forty-one. He was a Special Agent in the FBI and an operator on the elite Hostage Rescue Team. He was killed alongside a fellow operator on a maritime counterterrorism training mission. For years I have had a mother's premonition that I would lose him. However, there is nothing that can prepare you for the loss of your child. The day our younger son came to inform us of Chris's death is burned into my memory, my heart, my soul. As I collapsed on the floor sobbing, I felt my heart disappear with him. I knew I could never let him go, and I believe he too knew; so he took most of me with him. I felt like an empty vessel, with my spirit floating away. A great abyss of darkness and sadness loomed before me, as I realized that as his mother, I would search for him forever.

Chris was extraordinary in every way. He was a gifted scholar, athlete, and natural leader. From an early age, his teachers commented that he was truly a deep thinker. Critical thinking was his forte, and striving for excellence his personal motto. There was nothing superficial about him, and he possessed a maturity beyond his years. His achievements were due to his discipline, planning, hard work and devotion, and attention to detail.

Chris loved being part of the FBI and HRT. He was happiest being with his fellow operators, serving his country. The men work so well together, because of their mutual respect and admiration. While there were many eulogies upon Chris's death noting his extraordinary skill as an operator, there was one that especially struck a chord with me. One operator noted that beyond his operator skill, Chris also somehow possessed the ability to make the Universe align to accomplish what was needed on any particular mission. No one could ever explain this mystical, magical skill that he demonstrated. Upon his death, he has continued to demonstrate this ability to somehow communicate with me in his own special way.

The minute I learned of Chris's death I stopped praying and was no longer so sure about God either. Everything changed in an instant. I was completely shattered and only wanted the pain to stop; I only wanted Chris to comfort me. Beginning just days after his passing, odd things began to happen. I didn't realize it at the time, but Chris was going to come to comfort me and he was going to take me on a journey to ease my pain and restore my faith.

Some of these experiences simply involved a very strong presence, others provided evidence that could be seen or touched. Whenever I had these experiences I felt a chill or a sense of surrealism. I think my first connection with Chris occurred at his wake when my husband, son, and I were standing at his casket. Our son, Jason, looked at his brother, clasped his hands in front, and bowed his head. At that moment I felt absolutely *compelled to say: "Jason, you are just as courageous as Chris. You literally picked me up off the floor and carried your Dad and me at the darkest time of our lives. Chris is so very proud of you."*

I know I felt that sentiment, but I really think it was Chris saying to me, "Mom, tell Jason now." Chris loved Jason so much. I know he wanted only the best for him and I know he was so proud of him, as his Dad and I are proud of him. I recalled a few years earlier when I jokingly told Chris that he would probably just "put me in a home in my old age." Chris suddenly got serious and remarked that Jason would be the one to take care of me. Perhaps this was his premonition that he would not be here.

As soon as we arrived home from Chris's formal memorial at Quantico I started to plan our Memorial in our hometown. There was such an outpouring of love and pride for Chris. However, each time I started my work I was faced with lights going out, printer failure, power failure and even a chipmunk that invaded my study where I was working on my computer. I finally said, "Chris, are you messing with me? Don't you want me to have this beautiful memorial for you? Do you want me just to rest? I can't do that; I am compelled to do this to honor you and give the community the opportunity to mourn you."

I went on to purchase some needed supplies and as I sat in my car at the stoplight, I glanced into my rearview mirror and saw Chris sitting in the car behind me. He was wearing glasses like he wore a few years ago. He kept looking straight at me with his head resting on his right fist; his head was slightly tilted as if in concentration and concern. (Later when my husband and I were watching old video tapes of Chris, I was astonished to see him resting his head on his right fist – just as he did when I saw him in the car). I wanted to run back to his car and hold him; but I thought if I did the person in the car would think I was absolutely crazy; or if I got out I might discover that it really didn't look like Chris at all. So I decided to savor the moment and just hold Chris in my sight.

In October my husband and I visited Chris's lake house. The fall colors were magnificent around the lake and I couldn't help but to think of Chris and recall how he pleased he would have been to have his dad and me enjoying his boat and the beauty of nature.

On our last morning at the lake house I awoke very early, just before dawn, and opened the drapery to see the sun trying to break through in the distance; there was a soft mist hovering over the lake. It was an incredible combination of light and darkness. I felt that Chris was with me there; trying to break through that bright early morning sun, the darkness all around, with the mist gently illuminating the lake. It was one of the most beautiful sites I had ever seen; it was magical, mystical and very spiritual. Chris wanted me to see the beauty in the world; just as I advised him in my last written communication to him: "The world is a beautiful place; stop and let it in." I think that he wanted to reassure me that he was still with me; and he loved me; and the world was still a beautiful place. See the light in the darkness. I felt his presence enfold me. I took several

pictures. Later when I had my digital pictures developed of that scene, I saw a bright orb of light shining through the darkness of the trees. I believe it was indeed Chris's spirit.

Chris continues to let me know he is still with me. One day I was fretting about not having any of the Christmas ornaments he made as a child, because our crawl space flooded years ago and ruined everything, As I wandered through the rooms, I opened a nightstand drawer and there right before my eyes was a picture frame he made out of wooden sticks that were glued together and stained to look like a wood frame. The frame held a picture of Chris who looked to be around eight years old. I put a gold string on it and gently placed on our Christmas tree. The following Christmas I was hanging the ornaments on the downstairs tree, when I found another ornament that Chris had made me. It was quite large: an 8" paper plate with macaroni sprayed gold on the back with Chris's Cub Scout picture on the front. How could I have missed finding this ornament last Christmas? I know I searched endlessly for a childhood ornament. Now I have two.

My grief counselor, a Catholic priest, once advised me that I was living in a 'state of grace' as Chris seemed to come to me in so many mystical ways. Recently, I was telling a friend about another instance where Chris intervened in my life. Finally, my friend said, "You always say you believe that God works through people. Yet since Chris's death, you have stopped praying and professed that you weren't so sure about God either. How do you know that all this comfort you have received from Chris isn't really coming from God?" This stopped me in my tracks; an epiphany occurred. For years I had been searching for Chris, and all this time Chris had been leading me back to God; to a better understanding of the Universe, death, resurrection and my own spirituality.

I am a completely changed person. I have undergone a true spiritual awakening, all due to my journey with Chris. He brought me a gift.

It has been nearly three years since Chris's death. I have only dreamed of him twice. The first time I saw him skiing; he was smiling and happy. In the second dream, I had such a feeling of anger as my heart pounded. I was so enraged that Chris had been taken from me. Suddenly in this dream a man appeared; I didn't see his face, but he was dressed in an impeccable suit and I knew it was FBI Special Agent Chris. He slowly walked to me, and then enfolded me in his arms. I instantly felt a complete sense of peace and love. My anger disappeared.

Death and love are the two wings that bear the good man to heaven
—Michelangelo

One and Only Bears

All these instances of extraordinary encounters have offered opportunities to establish a new relationship with Chris; one that I believe is even stronger than the relationship I had with him when he was alive. I know that all these encounters are not just coincidences; these "coincidences" are therapeutic, an unbreakable link between the soul and the superior workings of the universe.

As Thornton Wilder writes in The Bridge of San Luis Rey, "There is a land of the living and the land of the dead. The bridge is love"

Grief is more than the pain of losing a loved one. Grief can take you on a unique journey that you never would have experienced otherwise. Grief can reveal all the miracles occurring every day; both the ordinary and extraordinary. Loved ones remind us of their presence by all the acts of kindness shown by people who strive to ease our pain. Extraordinary experiences exist outside the normal, if we look.

Our loved ones can take us on a journey where we discover the deeper meaning of life; an understanding of ourselves, our spirituality, and life after death...It is in this next life I will again embrace my beloved son, Christopher.—Janet

Prayer in communication with God is a safe and respectful outlet for our fears, feelings, frustrations, and thankfulness. Teddy bears are a little like God. They listen without judgment, and they are always there for us—if we let them be. Sometimes, it seems we're too busy or maybe we think we've outgrown them, and they get thrown aside as if they are no longer needed. Yet painful events or sorrowful times can draw us closer to God, or they can distance us. It is our choice. Just know that like a teddy bear, God is always there for you.

The Other Side

My husband, Jorge, and I have been together for close to twenty years. In that time, we have been through things that most people don't experience in an entire lifetime. The year 2007 was a very interesting year for a lot of people. For us, it was one of the most difficult years we had experienced together. There were a number of things that happened to us during that year, loss of our business, some serious health issues, losing our home, to name a few things. But the most difficult thing that happened was that our beloved dogs both passed away, on the same day. We had been together ten years at that point and since we didn't have any children, our dogs had become our family. The day that they went to Rainbow Bridge was the hardest thing that we had to go through up to that point in our marriage. Going home to an empty house was just heartbreaking. We cried so many tears and stared at their beds for long periods of time, hoping that it was just a bad dream. But unfortunately, it wasn't.

Life seemed to find its way back to normalcy as time went on. A few years had gone by and we were anxiously awaiting the arrival of our first baby! 2011 was shaping up to be our best year! At our thirty-seven-week appointment with our OB, we received news that would change our lives forever. The doctor was unable to find a heartbeat. Our baby boy had gone home to be amongst the angels. Words don't even come close to the feelings that Jorge and I had after that. All of our hopes, our dreams—gone.

With each of these losses there was a different kind of grieving and in turn different ways that we dealt with our healing and emotions. So much sadness, depression, longing, it was an all-encompassing feeling of despair that made it hard for us to think that it would ever end. We cried so many tears, and spent many days just wallowing around not knowing which way to turn or how to crawl out of this hole that we were in. We leaned on each other and spoke about the times that made us smile when the dogs were with us. Focusing on the positive things helped significantly in our healing. It was hard; I'm not going to lie, because there were days that we just wanted to stay in bed all day. But we pressed on, forcing ourselves to go through the motions until enough time had passed and our hearts had healed.

We also turned to faith and paralleled our lives to that of the Biblical story of Job. As we all know, after the trials that he went through, he was rewarded for his obedience and faith in abundance! Knowing and believing in this, made it somewhat easier for us to make it through. There would eventually be an end to this storm we were living and the sun would once again shine on us. Time is the best healer. The further you are from the event, the easier it is to deal with it. Understand that with loss, you will never get over it; you just learn to deal with it better.

Taking things one day at a time is key. Little victories should be enough in the beginning and should be celebrated. Things as small as taking a shower and getting dressed. To those not going through anything it may sound ridiculous, but to the person who has a hard time just getting out of bed is a huge deal!

There was a goal that we strived for every day, whether we achieved it or not didn't matter. The idea was to have one thing to work toward to keep us moving in the right direction. We did not put a deadline on when we should start feeling better and moving on. We cried when we felt sad, talked things out when we felt like we needed to talk. We kept those family and friends that we trusted close and removed those that weren't. This part was difficult for us, but so important! Surrounding yourself with positive and supportive people is so important. During such a delicate time, people sometimes say things that are so hurtful and can get in the way of your healing process.

These types of circumstances can really challenge a marriage. Thankfully, it brought Jorge and me closer together. We created a safe environment to talk about our innermost feelings without judgment or criticism.

Jorge and I know that there will be tough times ahead at some point in the future, but if we made it through those horrible storms of the past, we can certainly make it through whatever is to come. I have since been strong enough to help others that are going through things. I guess the more that I help others the better healed I become.

JJ Bear

One huge and very tangible part of our healing came when we had a teddy bear made in memory of our son JJ so we could store his ashes in. The same length and weight, wearing the outfit we were to bring him home in, and a recording of his heartbeat that I had from one of my doctor visits. It's amazing how real it feels to be able to hold my teddy bear and feel like I am holding my son. When our dogs died, we had a soft sculpture replica of each of them before they passed as well. Having our baby bear, and our doggie bears to hug and talk to and cry on was incredible! Even today, whenever we need a little extra comfort, we will hold our little JJ bear, or the dogs and sit on the couch and watch TV. We know that they are not a replacement for them not being with us, but it is certainly comforting. Everyone deals with their circumstances differently.

What worked for us, may not work for others, but the key to anyone going through hardship is to know that they are not alone and that happier times are just around the corner. It took us close to seven years to finally be able to smile at what we had been through. We could now talk to those in challenging times and to be an inspiration and motivating voice. We look back and know that times were unimaginably tough for us and at times it felt like we would never see the end, but we are now on the other side of that black cloud, and the future looks bright. —Mindy

I place no hope in my strength, nor in my works: but all my confidence is in God my protector, who never abandons those who have put all their hope and thought in Him.
—Francois Rabelais

Meditation

Meditation can help us embrace our worries, our fear, our anger; and that is very healing. We let our own natural capacity of healing do the work.—Thich Nhat Hanh

editation and yoga are two separate practices; however, they work beautifully and beneficially together. Yoga along with meditation techniques can help calm the mind by focusing on the way we breathe. This has long been known to lower blood pressure and help reduce stress. A study at the University of Wisconsin found that with consistent yoga practice, there is evidence of lower rates of depression. This occurs by stimulating a significant increase in serotonin levels and a decrease in the levels of cortisol and monoamine oxidase, an enzyme that breaks down our neurotransmitters. The MAO enzyme is responsible for breaking down and removing our happy hormones and endorphins.

This study also found that in everyone who meditated, the left prefrontal cortex showed enhanced activity, which correlated with greater levels of happiness and better immune function. Although this sounds a little scientific to me, it simply means that meditation and yoga can help make you not just feel better, but actually be better.

Breathing can play an effective role in calming, and put our mind at rest, not just in stressful situations, but on a daily basis. There are breathing techniques you can follow, or simply learn to take time to be mindful of your breathing, and practice awareness of your being.

A calming and effective breathing technique I use is may work for you: sit comfortably, close your eyes, and slowly and deeply inhale through your nose while counting to seven. Hold for seven seconds, and then release the air out of your slightly open mouth. Slowly let all your breath out, and take a little longer exhaling than you do inhaling. Breathe in deeply for seven seconds, hold for seven, and fully exhale out of your mouth. Try this seven times. Be sure to fully expand your lungs and then completely release all the air. You want the lungs and heart working optimally, sending fresh oxygen throughout your body.

The purpose of the counting is to keep your mind in the present and focused only on your being, rather than external or even internal stimuli. Practice a breathing technique anytime you feel agitated, discouraged, angry, or stressed. It will give you a few minutes of calmness and allow your body to naturally absorb stressors by reducing bad hormones and releasing endorphins and healthy hormones.

Meditating helps to have a thoughtless state of mind. Breathing helps calm, and prepare our mind for this awareness. Meditating regularly and consistently will provide the greatest benefit. However, any amount of time you dedicate to the calming of your mind, body, and spirit, will provide more positive direction than none at all.

It's very important that we re-learn the art of resting and relaxing. Not only does it help prevent the onset of many illnesses that develop through chronic tension and worrying; it allows us to clear our minds, focus, and find creative solutions to problems.—Thich Nhat Hanh

The purpose of life
is not to be happy.
It is to be useful,
to be honorable,
to be compassionate,
to have it make some
difference that you
have lived and
lived well.

—Ralph Waldo
Emerson

Giving

*F*orgiveness is the greatest form of giving we can offer. Forgiveness is peace, forgiveness is strength. Forgiveness is freedom from the pain that keeps one bound in a state of unrest. Forgiveness is hope.

Forgiving encompasses extending unconditional love and acceptance toward ourselves, or another that has wronged us—real or perceived. There may be nothing more uplifting and restoring for our spirit than forgiveness. Unforgiveness is one of the sharpest and cruelest thorns of emotional unrest in the hearts of people today, and so often, it goes unrecognized. It is a disease of the heart that will perpetually inflict emotional pain.

Forgiving someone doesn't mean we suddenly invite the person over for afternoon tea or play scrabble, but forgiving means we are no longer tethered to a source of pain, guilt or anger. Our heart is no longer bound in torment, and we are released from the hold the pain has on our heart. However, forgiving is not a single event, but a constant state of mind. We should strive to live in a continuous state of forgiveness. Forgiving releases space in our heart for greater peace, love, and hope.

If someone has hurt you or someone you love, forgiveness may not yet be a concept for you, and that's okay. Forgiveness cannot be forced; it must be experienced from the heart. There is a time and place for it, and it's not the same for everyone. No matter the wrongdoing, it is for our own spiritual and emotional well-being that we must keep our hearts open for forgiveness. Let's not allow someone else's bitterness to infect our own spirit. Keep an open heart; it may come when least expected.

Millie Me Bears

It's important to reflect on our relationships and make peace in our hearts. You have been hurt, I have been hurt. Whether past or present, real or perceived, we need to assure ourselves we are not holding grudges or resentments against those who have perpetrated that pain or judgment. I refuse to let the past rob me of my joy today and of my tomorrows. Have a spirit of forgiveness, and let us not forget, sometimes the person that we most need to forgive is ourselves.

Harnessed bitterness will only manifest into anger—that hurts you most. Understand that forgiveness and understanding someone's brokenness doesn't mean you accept or condone their behavior, it means that you know that they are a flawed individual and can empathize with why they may be. It releases you from the clutches of anger that can drive us into darkness. —M.H.

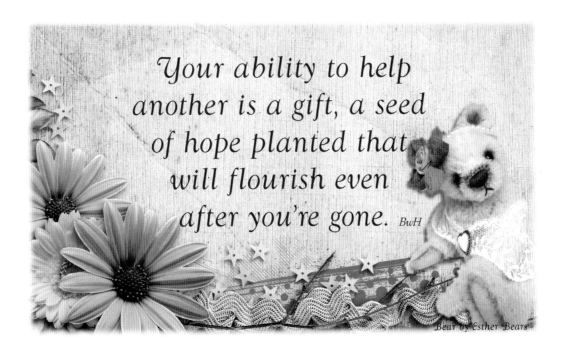

Your ability to help another is a gift, a seed of hope planted that will flourish even after you're gone. BwH

Bear by Esther Bears

Sharing our Heart, our Hands, and our Hope

When we make it our purpose to help others, to encourage others, to love others, our joy will simply be a natural, organic response to the seeds of hope we plant. When we provide another that which we need, we have given our life purpose beyond measure. Helping another in need, or in pain is the surest way to make lives better, lights shine brighter and hearts heal more fully.

When I do good, I feel good. When I do bad, I feel bad.
—Abraham Lincoln

When we extend compassion, kindness, and hope to others, our cup will always be full. When you are feeling lonely, visit someone in the VA hospital, children's center, nursing home, or the animals at a pet shelter. If you feel unappreciated or taken for granted, extend gratitude to those you appreciate, write a letter of thankfulness or send a goodie-filled gift basket to someone you truly appreciate. Offer to others that which you are in need of, or missing in your own life.

Millie Ann Bears

Happy people find joy in giving. If you have the means, search out a worthy cause, something that you are passionate about and offer what you are able. My passion has always been in helping the homeless, both humankind and dog-kind. What might be close to your heart? Look to your own community, find a need and fill it. This kindness will in turn fill your heart, and another heart with joy.

> Generosity is not giving me that which I need more than you do, but it is giving me that which you need more than I do.—Khalil Gibran

One and Only Bears

If I can't give tangibles, I can give a little of my time, it can be more valuable and meaningful to me, as well as the recipient. There are many opportunities to make a difference—I can read to the elderly, volunteer, be a mentor, walk a shelter dog, or simply pray for another. There are many ways within my own community to make a difference, and if I can make a difference in one person's life, then I have created a little hope and planted a seed that will flourish beyond myself.

Within a couple of weeks after Mom's death, I resumed my studies at the University of Oklahoma where I was working on my undergraduate degree in psychology. As fate would have it, shortly into one of the lectures we started a chapter on death and dying. I thought, *"Okay, Tammy, you can do this, you can handle this."* However, within minutes, the tears flowed and I couldn't see to write or even hear what was being said. I quietly left the classroom and found the nearest restroom to be alone. I leaned up against the wall and slowly sank to the floor; I just sat there and cried. After a moment, there was a hand on my shoulder that brought me back to where I was. I looked up and saw a young woman, not more than twenty years old, who sat down beside me on the bathroom floor without saying a word.

Somehow, she knew words were insufficient at that moment. She didn't try to make me feel better by offering up the usual platitudes. She was just there. She was present, she gave me her time. And *that* did make me feel better. Often, I look back at that day and wonder if she was even real; maybe she was an angel.

Bear with one another in love.—Ephesians 4:2

A Widow's Heart

On October 12, 2006, three words changed my life forever. Following my husband's endoscopy, the doctor pulled me into a private room, and his first words to me were "Not good news." They had discovered a four-inch tumor in his esophagus. He was diagnosed with esophageal cancer and given a prognosis of one year (I never told him this). The world suddenly ended. He was determined to fight it, but I plunged into a deep depression complete with anxiety attacks with an all-consuming fear of how I was ever going to make it on my own. I sought help for my depression and was finally able to be the support for him that I needed to be.

I was grateful for this year because it gave me the opportunity to do many of the simple things that are often taken for granted in a relationship (like saying I love you every day), and we grew closer than ever. I was his primary caregiver and God gave me the strength to do things I never thought I could do. He fought so hard, and suffered so much, and after chemo, radiation, surgeries, numerous hospital stays, his earthly battle was not to be won. Hospice was called and he went home to die. He passed away peacefully on October 19, 2007. A hole was ripped in my heart so big that I thought it would never beat normally again.

After a three month absence, I returned to work, which was a saving grace for me because during the time I was there, I had to think about something else. I was blessed to have wonderful support from my family, friends, co-workers, and church family. I have two wonderful daughters (who are also very much missing their dad). I think that a turning point in my grief occurred when one day a thought popped into my head—my husband is gone, but I'm still here. God must not be finished with me yet. I prayed that he would show me what I was supposed to do with the rest of my life. One answer didn't take that long to come. I worked for a credit union, and somehow all of these recently widowed women ended up at my window. I found this out just through casual conversations with them, and when I mentioned that I was in a similar situation, many of them poured their hearts out to me. I did the only thing that needed to be done. I listened. I think that this helped me as much as it did them, knowing that we shared this bond and were not alone.

I retired in 2012 and had already decided on one thing that I wanted to do. Although my husband only received hospice care for four days before he passed, I was so impressed with the care and compassion showed to him and my family by the caregivers of that organization, that I wanted to be a part of them, so I signed up to be a volunteer. I also signed up to be a volunteer at the food pantry that operates out of my church. I am a crafty person by nature, but as a result of a card making class that I took, I found out that I was given the gift of being able to create cards that people find special enough to buy. I have started my own card business, but mostly, I make cards to donate to sell as a fundraiser for hospice, as a thank you for the wonderful work that they do.

The last 8 ½ years have been sometimes challenging, often scary and lonely, but also full of experiences and people who have come into my life that might have not otherwise have happened. Much has been taken from me, but much has been given back, and although life will never be the same as it was, it will be what I make it. I am still grieving (grief has no timetable), for to not have grieved means to not have loved. But I am also living. I am still here and whatever plans God has for the rest of my life will be revealed to me. He made a promise to me in my favorite Bible verse (Jeremiah 29:11): "For I know the plans I have for you, says the Lord. They are plans for good and not for disaster, to give you a future and a hope." And I believe it—Janice

Two Dollars...Priceless

Some time ago, I was having a really bad day. I was going through a difficult stretch and was easily agitated with the smallest of things. If I could see it, smell it, or touch it, it annoyed me. And to further my angst, I needed to go to the grocery store to pick up some necessities. I arrived at the store, and the parking lot was full. I got a buggy that squeaked. I got in line and waited—and waited. I was practicing the R in my CPR, but I wasn't succeeding, my arteries were getting clogged. My thoughts were negative and angry. The cashier asked how I was doing. I wanted to say, "You really don't want to know!"

Your joy comes from what you give, not what you accumulate.
—Frank C. Laubach

Instead, I forced a smile and said, "Okay, thank you." I paid, and out the door I went with a young man pushing my groceries just behind me. He was kind, courteous, and carefully loaded the groceries in the trunk. When he finished, I handed him a tip—his face lit up as if I'd just handed him a hundred dollars. He seemed so happy to receive a tip. It was only a couple of dollars, but it clearly meant a lot to him. Connecting to his reaction instantly opened up my Heart, and it was through the act of giving that the flow of hope and peace came flooding through. My drive home was filled with a sense of purposefulness and joy. Amazing what a few dollars can buy.

Denise Purrington Bears

If you learn from your suffering, and really come to understand the lesson you were taught, you might be able to help someone else who's now in the phase you may have just completed. *Maybe that's what it's all about after all.—Anonymous*

Not what we say about our blessings, but how we use them, is the true measure of our thanksgiving.—W.T. Purkiser

Skye Rose Bears

Gratitude

*We must find time to stop and thank the people
who make a difference in our lives.
—John F. Kennedy*

Every minute is truly a gift. We are given the opportunity to be grateful despite the challenges we are faced with. Gratefulness does not come only from a happy heart, but happiness comes from a grateful heart. A heart full of gratitude is also a heart full of joy. When we hurt, it's helpful to be mindful of all that we can be thankful for. It won't take away the pain, but it can help deal with grief and sorrows with a lighter and more hopeful heart.

Many words in the English language have different meanings; one of those words is "present." Present has three meanings:

- ♥ Firstly, *present* means to be *here*
  In school the teacher would take roll and we would answer with either *here* or *present.*
- ♥ Secondly, it means *now*
  At the *present* moment, you are reading this right *now.*
- ♥ Lastly, it means a *gift*
  I want to give you a *present* because I love you.

It seems there is something to this. Right *here*, right *now* is a *gift.* We shouldn't fret over the past, nor should we fear the future. What we have is the *here* and *now,* and it is truly a *gift* to be thankful for.

When we are going through tough times, it's the best time to be mindful of all that we are thankful for. Restoring and re-directing our thoughts on to the positive in our lives, is what will help push us forward.

Here is a short list of some of the people and things, both little and big I am thankful for.

- ♥ All Life
- ♥ My husband and our dogs
- ♥ Family and friends
- ♥ My mental and physical health
- ♥ My left hand *and* my little right nub
- ♥ Our service men and women, police forces, and our firefighters
- ♥ Teachers, professors, and scientists
- ♥ Doctors, emergency workers, and veterinarians
- ♥ The mountains
- ♥ Our home, clothes, food —things often taken for granted
- ♥ Nature—the trees, flowers, wildlife, birds, and butterflies...even the ants and spiders
- ♥ Ice cream and coffee
- ♥ Football and basketball
- ♥ Each of you who are reading this book

*I*t's important to think about who we personally appreciate by putting a face on the people we are thankful for. Consider the firefighters who would respond to our home if needed or the police and emergency workers that would be called to our aid in case of an accident. Be thankful for your fifth-grade teacher, or your child's fifth-grade teacher. The veterinarian who saved your dog's life or the care provider who went the extra mile when you needed it most. Finding ways to not only experience and feel gratefulness, but putting actions with our thankfulness is what will fill our heart, and another heart, with joy. How can I let them know how much they mean to me? Here are a few thoughtful ways to consider showing gratitude to those who mean so much.

- ♥ Thank them with a handwritten card
- ♥ Have flowers, fruit, or a candy basket delivered
- ♥ Call them and listen
- ♥ Personally take them a plate of cookies or a cake

Thinking of others is a beautiful way to restore our own thoughts from negative to something positive. Hopeful, happy people feel gratitude for everything from the greatest to the smallest of things; this connects us with others and provides our heart with purpose and hope.

The Glove

When Marc and I divorced in 2001, I decided to follow a dream we had held together, to move to Colorado. We had often talked about moving there and opening up a gift shop or a Bed & Breakfast; things always got in the way of following those dreams. The day our divorce was final, I packed the car, and with my new little schnauzer, Pico, riding shotgun, we headed to Colorado.

It was a bold step, but one I took with optimism and hope. I had goals and a plan to achieve those goals. I found a charming old house right on the main street and opened a little gift shop I named The Bear Hug.

Pico and I would regularly take short drives after closing shop for the day. He loved the ride, and I loved the mountain drive. Something about the mountains provided me a peaceful place in my heart and in my mind.

One day after I closed up, as usual, I was readying for our drive, but this time, I decided not to take Pico. I felt I wanted to be alone that evening. We recently had a big snow come through and the mountains were gloriously covered. Although I was new to the town, I felt comfortable driving the area and the main roads were always well maintained even with the recent snows. That evening, I knew right where I wanted to drive, it was a road that looped around the entire town from one side to the other, and was a magnificent, scenic drive.

After what seemed like several miles into my drive, I noticed my surroundings weren't looking as familiar as they should, and the road seemed to have gotten, well, snowy. Somehow, while my soul was relishing the peaceful surroundings, I wasn't being mindful of the fact the roads weren't quite so well maintained, and I was completely enveloped in the snow-covered forest. It was then I realized I wasn't where I thought I was. I wasn't on the loop, but I had accidentally taken the fork, a forest road that took me up the mountain, not around town.

Before I could even find a way to turn around, I was stuck. I tried to get out of the rut I was in; I found rocks, sticks, and even put my car mats behind the back wheels to try to gain traction, but all to no avail. After a while, I reconciled to myself that my car wasn't going anywhere, but by then, what *was* going somewhere was the daylight. I really wasn't sure how far out and up the road I was. I had been driving slowly, and it could have been two or ten miles, I wasn't sure. I sat in the car awhile pondering how I had gotten myself into that predicament.

I gathered my thoughts, strength, coat, hat, and gloves and decided to walk back to the loop, which, isn't a main road, but at least I would know how far out I was and could mentally prepare for the walk. I wasn't counting on anyone driving by unless it was an out-of-towner who doesn't know any better than to stay off the roads after a snowstorm.

By that time it was dark, and in January in the mountains, nighttime fell earlier than what I was accustomed to. But to my wonderment, the stars peeking through low clouds were acting as tiny little beacons, providing just enough reflection off the snow for my eyes to see a path. I was in the mountains; there were no streetlights, house lights, or car

lights. It was amazingly beautiful and serene with nothing but the complete stillness of the night. The only thing I could hear was my breath and an occasional crack of a tree branch breaking from the weight of the snow.

After a while, I began to get really cold, and with every breath I took, my lungs hurt more and more. I could barely feel my legs. I wasn't sure how far I'd walked; I just knew I was becoming increasingly colder and weaker. In Colorado, at 8,500 feet elevation, it could've easily been near or below zero by that time. I was so tired and cold and it seemed my walking was fruitless. My hope of a rescue, or at least finding the loop, seemed further and further away.

I began to reflect on my life, on the struggles I'd been through, the choices I'd made, both good and bad (one of which was driving that snowy road). I thought about Mama, and how much I missed her. I thought about Marc, about how much I still loved him, although we divorced, our relationship remained close.

I was so numb and weak I began thinking I could actually die. Was I happy with where, and who I was? What things could or should I be doing differently? Was I making a difference? Being so exhausted, I considered curling up next to a tree and just going to sleep. Knowing it would drop below zero during the overnight hours I wondered if I would even wake up, or be so frostbitten I'd lose the only five fingers I had.

Needing to rest, I lay down in the middle of the road and looked up at the sky. There was a scant low covering of clouds, but I could still see the stars and the silhouette of the forest trees. Then thoughts of Pico came to mind. He was back home locked up in his crate; I couldn't abandon him! My mind started racing. If I were to give up and possibly die, I may not be found for several days or longer. There wasn't anyone who would even report me missing! I regained my strength, both mentally and physically, and stood up to get back to Pico. But before I could resume my walk, I realized I was disoriented; I did not know which way I had been going, nor which way I had come from! It all looked the same. I looked one way, and then looked the other and began to cry. I didn't know which way to go. Curling up next to a tree crossed my mind again, but then I pushed through my anguish and began walking anyway. I wanted to get home to Pico and was determined not to die up there.

After walking a short while, I still wasn't sure if I was backtracking or moving forward. Looking for anything that seemed familiar, when in front of me I saw something small and dark in the middle of the road. I reached down to see what it was. It was a glove. But not just any glove—it was my glove. I was walking the direction from which I'd come. Not knowing if I wanted to cry or rejoice, I chose to rejoice and began to be ever so thankful for the glove I had just found. Although I wore a glove on my hand and another on my little nub, this one must have been an extra tucked somewhere. Since I have only one hand, I don't always carry gloves in pairs! I hadn't been backtracking very far, so with new hope and a surge of adrenaline, I headed back down the mountain.

After what seemed to be hours, I finally made it to the fork in the road, and within only a minute, a truck passed by and stopped to see if I needed help. It was a man and his son who just by happenstance were heading back toward town after being at a birthday party much later than they intended. They told me there wasn't another car on the road, and if I hadn't been right where I was at that time, I would have missed them. I thought about my backtracking, if I had not gone the wrong direction, the exact distance I did, I wouldn't have been there at that place for them to rescue me. When I got back to the house and with Pico, I was so thankful to be home, to be alive. By that time, it was after midnight. The whole ordeal only lasted about eight hours, but it seemed an eternity.

My trip up the mountain was just a small event in my life, but it provided me with a new appreciation for perseverance and a realization that I am where I am meant to be. Looking back, I highly doubt I would have frozen to death, though I might have suffered a smidgen of frostbite, but it certainly gave me cause to be grateful for everything and everyone in my life. It wasn't long after that Marc and I reconciled and re-committed our lives to each other.

Wednesday, September 13, 1995

Mom hasn't been able to get out of bed, it hurts too bad, and she's been coughing a lot. I laid down beside her again and rubbed her tummy, she's had a lot of nausea. When I was little she always rubbed my tummy when I was sick or not feeling good. I read to her from the book of John today. I brushed some hair off her face and just looked at her. Mom said, "Now Tammy, if something happens to me, I don't want you to cry too much. When you start crying just say, 'why am I crying for? Mom's in a beautiful place now.'

Words

Too often we underestimate the power of a touch, a smile, a kind word, a listening ear, an honest compliment, or the smallest act of caring, all of which have the potential to turn a life around.—Leo Buscaglia

I remember the childhood chant, "Sticks and stones may break my bones but words will never hurt me." However this could not be further from the truth. Words do matter.

Say you have a beautiful picture you want to hang on the wall. You find the perfect place for it, hammer in a few nails, and voila! It's perfect. But after you take a few steps back, you decide you don't like it there, so you remove the nails, hammer in a few more, and hang the picture back up. Thankfully, one of the nail holes is covered by the picture, but you'll have to use a filler to cover up the other holes. It's really perfect this time, you can't even see your mistake. However, despite being covered, the holes are still there, and they have permanently scarred the wall.

So it is with words. Once we put them in the wrong place, we can't take them back. Complaining and saying negative things only defeats our purpose of finding hope and happiness. It takes the same amount of energy to complain and be negative as it does to be positive and compliment. And being negative drains us of energy, while being positive builds you, me, and others up. A kind word might just give someone the hope they need to feel it's going to be okay, and that, in return, just might give you the hope you need to know it's going to be okay.

This Too...

As a teenager in my high school sophomore year, I had no confidence. I had a disapproving father who was critical and yelled at me constantly, "You're stupid!" I was timid, socially awkward and painfully shy. Life for me at age fifteen was unbearable. At school, shyness and low self-esteem stopped me from talking and interacting with classmates and peers. I was a loner, an outsider. During lunch, I would sit alone hiding behind a book as everyone else talked and laughed, having normal social exchanges. I wished I was normal.

At home, there was yelling, fights, criticism and ridicule. I had nowhere to turn for peace, for solace. I began drinking daddy's ever-present wine, even sneaking it to school and drinking in class. I'd skip school two days a week and go shoplifting at the local stores. I would steal clothes, jewelry, things I wanted but couldn't afford, plus lots of candy and ice cream. Then I'd eat until I hurt. My life was an endless nightmare with no hope of it ever ending.

 Every day after school, I rode my yellow Suzuki 100 to the local cemetery. I'd walk through the old headstones, then sit on the ground under a big oak tree, staring at the sky and ponder life's meaning. What was it all about? Why was I here? How could I escape the pain? I saw only two options—I could run away or I could kill myself. I played each one out in my head. If I killed myself, it would be over. Period. The end. There would be no going back. If I ran away, I was too young to get a real job. How could I support myself? I'd have to be a hooker and sell myself. But how could I tell the guy to pay me? I was so shy I couldn't even talk to a boy. How could I...even if I could...how could I possibly ask for money? I can imagine him laughing in my face and saying, "You weren't any good! I'm not paying you a cent!"

Back at school, my history teacher, Mr. Robbins, was a fifty-year-old, bald-headed guy with a little gray fuzz above his ears. He was good-natured and jovial, always cracking jokes and making the class fun and interesting. The popular kids would joke around with him, usually something involving his bald head.

They had the self-confidence to talk, to tell jokes, to interact with authority figures. I didn't. I loved Mr. Robbins, but I couldn't say one word to him.

Occasionally when students got out of hand or weren't listening, his temper came out. Nostrils flaring, he glared over his wire-rimmed glasses, and we knew it was serious. He would whip them off  and fling them onto his desk. Then we'd be at the receiving end of a good rant. The class would straighten up fast. It never took long for Mr. Robbins to get back to his usual good-humored self.

Day after day, I'd sit at the cemetery, growing more desperate, running scenarios through my tortured mind. Should I kill myself? Should I run away? One day sitting in history class waiting for Mr. Robbins to arrive, everyone around me chatted noisily. I stared at my open book wishing he would appear so that my silence wouldn't be so resounding. When he finally entered, he did something he'd never done before. He walked straight to the blackboard, picked up chalk and wrote,

"This too soon shall pass."

Without acknowledging what he wrote, he walked to his desk, opened the history book and began his lecture. Spellbound, I stared at the board as the words reverberated through my head, "This too soon shall pass. This too soon shall pass." I read it over and over and over. Its meaning and *significance slowly made its way into my black and dismal world. I grabbed hold of it as if it was a life raft thrown to me in a vast, raging ocean.*

The meaning of those words was everything to me. If this too shall pass, I reasoned to myself, then the hell I was going through would pass, too. I clung desperately to those words. I was drowning and Mr. Robbins had just thrown me a life vest. He saved my life that day. Very soon after that, my life got better. I got a part-time job and I made friends who liked and accepted me, which helped me to come out of my shell. I never told Mr. Robbins, but the day he wrote that quote on the board, he saved the life of a lost and lonely young girl who couldn't see a way out.

Throughout my life, through some of the darkest times, those words have come back to me, giving me hope, helping me to believe that things will get better. And I tell others the same thing. When I know someone is going through a difficult time, I tell them, "This too soon shall pass. Things always get better." Mr. Robbins, you never knew it, but I loved you for that. I'm sorry I never told you.

Not only did Shelia express a grateful heart for Mr. Robbins, she also took the words that gave her hope and has paid them forward to others in discouraging times. Words can change the outlook of someone hurting, they don't have to be prophetic or profound, but just be kind, gracious and sincere. We have the power to make a difference, and sometimes that power is just within words.

It was about a year after Mama's death, I found myself at another funeral. My cousin Harold, lost his life in a house fire—he was just forty-one years old. One morning shortly before dawn, he glanced out his back window and saw the home behind his engulfed in flames. The home belonged to his son, daughter-in-law, and their two young children. I cannot begin to imagine the terror that arose in his heart. Without hesitation, he courageously ran into the blaze to rescue his family. Not only did he lose his life, tragically, all five perished in the fire.

After the service, I remember approaching my cousin's wife just to hold her hand, to give her a hug. Although we were never close and had not seen each other in many years, one of the first things she said to me was that she was so sorry about my mama's passing. It took all I had to not break down into tears. It was surreal—I was at a funeral with multiple caskets, one of which her two grandbabies shared, and she selflessly had the mindfulness to offer me compassion. Her thoughtfulness and words touched me so deeply, they have stayed with me all these years.

Did I offer peace today?
Did I bring a smile to
someone's face?
Did I say words of healing?
Did I let go of my anger
and resentment?
Did I forgive? Did I love?
These are the real questions.
I must trust that the little bit
of love that I sow now will
bear many fruits, here in this
world and the life to come.
—Henri Nouwen

Thursday, Sept 14, 1995

I fixed Mom some chicken and
dumplings, it didn't turn out
so great, but Mom being mom
said it was just fine. I told her
I wished I had something better
to fix her. "It wouldn't hurt"
she replied with a coy grin
on her face. We both
laughed out loud
and then laughed
some more.

Laughter

I never would have made it if I could not have laughed. It lifted me momentarily out of this horrible situation just enough to make it livable.—Viktor Frankl, Holocaust survivor

Laughing is letting go. When times are tough, it can seem impossible to have reason to laugh. While it is normal to mourn a loss and be frustrated with situations, it is also okay to experience a little happiness through some good humor and laughter.

Laughter produces a significant physiological change in our body and brain. It does the heart good, but it also does the mind and body good. It strengthens the immune system by increasing activity among immune cells and antibodies. It helps reduce physical pain and improves heart health by increasing blood flow and blood vessel function. Laughter releases tension by reducing those pesky stress-related hormones and releasing the endorphins responsible for increasing our sense of pleasure, which elevates our feelings and mood. Laughter simply evokes an overall sense of well-being (University of Maryland, July 2009).

While the laughter may only last a few minutes, the effects can last for hours. Cancer Treatment Centers of America has also made laughter therapy available as part of their complementary treatment regimens.

Patients have reported things such as, "I didn't even think about cancer during Laughter Club" and "Things have been so hard that we hadn't laughed in months." One doctor reported an eight-year-old daughter of a patient who attended Laughter Club said afterward, "I never thought about laughing every day, but now I realize I can. Like even when I don't feel happy, I can still laugh and feel better."

I remember the first time I enjoyed a meal and laughed soon after Mama died. My husband and I were dining at a restaurant with his mother and sister. As we waited for our dinner, we visited and talked about this or that. Something was said, and I laughed. I can't even remember what was said or who said it, but I do remember laughing. And I remember for a split second, I felt guilty—I questioned myself about how I could be laughing when Mom's life had been so painfully cut short. But it was also at that moment that I realized this is what Mama would want for me.

The laughter began my road to remembering her with joy and love, and no longer with pain and sorrow. The tears still flow, but they are tears of hope and of overcoming my grief. I don't grieve her death anymore, but celebrate her life. However, I will always miss her, and occasionally, my tears still flow as if her death was yesterday.

So let us laugh. What makes you smile? Kittens or puppies? A baby giggling? The shenanigans of kittens could make a statue laugh—and the innocence and playfulness of puppies can make me laugh till I'm crying again. And watching a video of a baby laughing, well, in my opinion, it just doesn't get any better than that. In a time of discouragement, open up your heart to joy. With the Internet, we have laughter at our fingertips. Watch some silly and sweet videos of these little critters and just get lost in their innocence and joyfulness. It will do your heart good.

Laugh, and laugh some more. Find a good comedy and watch with someone you love, your dog, or even your teddy bear. Sharing laughter is healing for the heart. Share funny stories of your children, siblings, or of your beloved one. Laugh at yourself for something silly you did or said. Just laugh, and soon you will find your road to overcoming hurts, with your heart a little lighter and your path a little brighter.

Thursday, September 14, 1995

I visited Mom today after class, she was really sad. Pop had tried to help her get up so she could walk, but her pain was worse than anything she could ever have imagined. She couldn't sit up, she just asked him to leave her alone awhile, she told me she cried for thirty minutes. I don't like talking about how much pain Mom is in, but I also don't want to forget how much she suffers, yet she keeps her faith and stays strong. I sat with her awhile and then just out of the blue she says, "I'm broke, your sister's broke, you're broke—it's awful how we're all broke at the same time"—after a long pause—"not really sure what we'd do with money anyway!" We both burst out in laughter.

It is well known that humor, more than anything else in the human make-up, can afford aloofness and an ability to rise above any situation, even if only for a few seconds.—Viktor Frankl

Friday, September 15, 1995

...Mom and I laughed again about how awful my chicken and dumplings were...

Mama could always find joy, even through the depth of her pain.

Thursday, October 21, 1995

I switched Mom from AT&T to Sprint last month and now AT&T called wanting her to switch back. They offered $15 plus 50% off all calls for three months, so I said sure, why not, knowing Mom could use the $15. I told Mom that yesterday. Today she told me that in the middle of the night last night that she thought about getting that $15 and she laughed—out loud. She got a kick out of it, she said we could just keep switching, then she laughed some more.

Beautiful Music
is the
Art
of the Prophets
that can
calm the agitations
of the
Soul;
It is one
of the most
magnificent
and
delightful presents
God
has given us

—Martin Luther

Music

Music can minister to minds diseased, pluck from the memory a rooted sorrow, raze out the written troubles of the brain, and with its sweet oblivious antidote, cleanse the full bosom of all perilous stuff that weighs upon the heart.—William Shakespeare

Music is considered by many to be the universal language of man-kind. It has been used for centuries to enhance both emotional and physical health and happiness. Music can help balance hormones, boost the release of endorphins, and provide a greater sense of peace and well-being.

Apollo, Plato, Aristotle, and Socrates all expressed their belief and desire for music to be part of emotional and physical healing. Plato referred to music as "the medicine of the soul" and believed that music had a powerful effect on our emotional states. Aristotle taught that music affects the soul and described music as a force that purified the soul by removing negative emotions. Hippocrates played music for those who suffered depressed moods. Music therapy was practiced in biblical times, when David played the harp to help King Saul when he was feeling disturbed or melancholy.

Whether it is listening, singing, or playing—music is hope and healing for the soul. And not surprisingly, studies bear the fact that music is good for both body and mind. Research supports that listening to music lowers heart rate, reduces the cortisol in our body, increases the flow of endorphins, and calms our mind (MacDonald, 2012).

After World Wars I and II, musicians would travel to hospitals and play music for soldiers suffering from both emotional and physical trauma. When the doctors noticed a measurable improvement in the patients' physical and emotional states, this opened the way for music therapy as we know it today.

(AMTA http://www.musictherapy.org/about/history)

Me and My Guitar

Music is like food and water to me. Playing guitar has been the only way I've been able to express myself, and to let myself feel. There were times the only thing I had was my music. The only thing I could count on. I've made a lot of poor choices, and bad decisions that cost me friendships and my family. I was broken, I abused alcohol and drugs, isolated myself, and finally I tried counseling, but none worked. Through the lowest times in my life, I reached for my music, and the music was always there for me, it has been my hope. I could always count on music helping me through. At times, it was the only thing that helped me to even breathe. After suffering in loneliness for far too long, with music searing through my soul, I was able to get back on my feet again. It somehow encouraged me and helped build my confidence to believe in myself again. I was able to make new friends, and made peace with my family. Music saved my life.—Jason

In the United States, Native American medicine men employed chants and dances as a method of healing patients.

Reduces Stress & Anxiety

When music is an integral part of our life we increase our body and mind's ability to positively improve our mood and lower stress levels. A doctoral thesis from the University of Gothenburg (Helsing, 2012) reveals that listening to music every day lowers stress by reducing the hormone cortisol. It also stirs up positive emotions, which is critical for our overall physical and psychological well-being. It's an effortless and effective way to lower stress and anxiety.

Researchers from Drexel University found that cancer patients who either listened to music or worked with a music therapist experienced a reduction in anxiety. This study found that people who participated in music somehow not only had less anxiety, but also better blood pressure levels and improved moods.

A Song for Me

A few years ago I was going through a deep depression. I was having relationship difficulties and I had no family or friends to turn to for support. Most times I would just cry and feel like I couldn't stop. I couldn't concentrate, and began to fail at work and in the college classes I was taking. I just wanted to be happy, but all I was, was angry and full of despair. I turned to alcohol to numb the pain, and put myself in risky and dangerous situations. I really didn't care if something happened to me. I just wanted to drink myself away. When I was at my lowest, when I thought nothing could help, I heard a song. It was a beautiful song, and it really wasn't the words, it was the music, the melody. I begin listening to it all the time, it somehow, someway made me feel better. It reached deep into my soul. I can't explain it. It lifted my spirit and encouraged me like nothing else had. It helped me to feel again. I had hope. I made the choice to accept the things I could not change, but also, accept that there were things I could choose to do that would make a difference. With music as my guide, I started making choices to do better for myself, music turned my life around. Music, saved me from myself.—Alison

Music washes away from the soul the dust of everyday life.

—Berthold Auerbach

Three O'Clock Bears

Improves Heart Health & Soothes Pain

University of Maryland Medical Center researchers have found a link between listening to music and heart health The researchers found that listening to joyful music is linked with dilation of blood vessels' inner lining, meaning more flow of blood through the blood vessels. Specifically, the diameter of blood vessels grew by 26 percent when a person listened to happy music. These results are almost parallel to their research on the effects of laughter. These studies show that listening to music isn't just an emotional response, but an actual physiological response that will enhance our overall well-being.

Researchers from the University of Utah Pain Research Center (*Journal of Pain*, 2011) showed that listening to music is effective when used as a distraction for people with severe anxiety. It also works as a diversion from feeling pain, and as a result, can actually help people feel less pain. Brain scans also support the finding that when we listen to music, the parts of our brain associated with pleasure are stimulated.

My mother was in tremendous physical pain once the cancer metastasized to her bones. No amount of pain medication could ease her physical pain. However she loved to listen to her gospel music, and she loved to sing it as well. Although the music didn't heal her physically, it nurtured her spiritual needs and provided mental and emotional moments of relief from her incomprehensible pain. It lifted her above the pain and into a place of peace and of hope.

One good thing about Music, when it hits you, you feel no pain.
—Bob Marley

Thursday, September 7, 1995

Mom was really sad today. Her left leg and back was really hurting. I rubbed her belly and told her I loved her. She started crying. Mom thought she was getting better but she said today was really bad. She said it feels like "glass gouging my bones". But she wants to get up and do things. She tried to sit up on the bed so she could French braid my hair. I told her no, but she insisted, she wanted to fix my hair like she used to. Despite the pain, she braided my hair. I never want to let this braid out. She sang, her voice is so beautiful. She feels close to God when she sings, she feels peace and says she receives a blessing. "How Great Thou Art" is her favorite, she really feels the Spirit, and so do I.

*H*aving music in our life opens up our heart for healing. Music isn't going to make our problems disappear or our pain go away, however it will provide moments of mental rest, comfort and peace. These are special moments that can help keep us moving forward and toward a better and brighter place—in our mind, and in our heart.

© John Bindon Art

Music affects the mind, body and soul in a very powerful, almost inexplicable way. Whatever our needs are, we can calm our spirit, stir up a joy in our heart, and experience peace at the inner most level.

Hope for the Day (HFTD) is a Chicago-based nonprofit organization that focuses on suicide prevention and mental health education through self-expression. It focuses on art and music to achieve outreach, education, and prevention. HFTD has a special video series, "Music Saved My Life," featuring internationally recognized musicians and artists who share their personal stories of struggling with suicide, depression, and mental illness.

Hope for the Day's vision is *to bring communities together in order to shed light on the unfortunate topics of depression and suicide.* Their desire is to *share the deeply personal connection that creativity can have in fostering an environment of positive change to those suffering.*

HFTD views art and music as a highway to the heart; two things that have allowed people to express their emotions for millennia. They strive to reduce suicide rates while inspiring and empowering those who need help, to get help. Most importantly: *We have the vision to use creative expression as a medium to educate communities while simultaneously striving to prevent suicide.*

It's ok not to be ok, have hope. (www.HFTD.org)

Music touches the spirit, frees the soul, opens the mind, and heals the Heart.

An excerpt from Grief: A Mother's Journey

Chris's death has left a path of devastation. Every day is such an effort. Why does he keep pushing us on? He seems to insist that we live, while I know that "dying is easy; living is hard, very hard." Every day I awaken with a headache and body aches. My first thought is "Chris is gone; how will I struggle to get through another day?" I finally started to talk to Chris about how tired I was as I faced each day. I was so exhausted both physically and emotionally.

Several days after lamenting to Chris, I was invited to a piano concert by my friend, Mary, who is also a bereaved mother. This Jim Brickman concert had a therapeutic effect. While the palliative benefits of music therapy are well known, I never experienced this therapeutic effect personally.

The morning after the concert was the first day in many months that I awoke without headache or body pain. In addition, my first thought was not of my terrible loss of Chris and my dread of facing the day. My first thought was the "Rainbow" music I heard at the concert the night before: "Rainbow Connection" and "Somewhere Over the Rainbow." I just lay in bed pain free feeling a sense of peace and tranquility. It was magical and I had to wonder if Chris somehow had something to do with this too. —Janet

$\mathcal{T}$ake a music bath once or twice a week for a few seasons. You will find it is to the soul what a water bath is to the body.—Wendall Holmes

Nature

When feeling down, depressed or discouraged, take time out to be with nature. Sit by a tree, smell a flower, watch a butterfly or hear the birds sing. Your spirit will be lifted, your heart will be opened, and you will feel better.

Nature provides breathtaking magnificence that touches us deeply through all of our senses. From crickets and birds chirping to raindrops falling, from the amazing beauty of the majestic mountains to a single leaf or pine cone; nature fills our senses with awe and wonder. It is our senses which keep us grounded, keep us connected to creation, and keep us connected to each other.

Aside from the beauty nature provides through sight, sound and scent; it also does something physiologically to our body that helps promote positive emotions and well-being. When discouraged, we can look to nature and find something grand, or ever-so-small to marvel at and see its beauty and place in the world. We can find joy and calmness in feeling the raindrops on our face, the scent of a flower or the sound of bees buzzing or birds singing.

As much a treat nature is to our eyes, so it is to our ears. Studies show the sounds of nature also help reduce stress, anxiety, and promote positive emotions (Alvarsson et al., 2010). It could be the sound of a babbling brook, rustling leaves in the wind, birds chirping, thunder, or ocean waves that resonates with the natural vibrations of our body. The beauty and wonder experienced in nature connect with us on a deeper, intrinsic level.

Mom loved to walk along the creek bed and look for rocks; she would always find one that looked like a bird, an angel, or the face of Jesus. She also loved to make things out of the clouds, whether a face or a flower, Mama was good at using her mental creative ability. This was her hobby, but it also provided a sense of peace, and emotional healing.

A recent study from Stanford University finds that walking or just *being* in nature provides significant mental health benefits, specifically it lowers the risk for depression, reduces stress, boosts the immune system, increases energy levels as well as improve sleep. (G. Bratman, *June 2015*).

It does the mind, heart, and body good to spend time in nature; it brings us calmness and clarity as it helps propel us to a restful state of being. Nature restores our minds and spirits, and helps elevate our thoughts to a place of peace, harmony, and hope.

Monday, September 18, 1995

It rained today, it felt good, the air, the breeze. Mom said it reminded her of being in the apple orchards and coming in from the rain and into their cabin after harvesting the fruit. She said it felt so nice. Mom talks about going places, she wished the house had a covered porch so she could sit out in the rain. Or if she could only get up she would get in the van just to be outside in the rain. Mom loves nature, the trees, the rocks, the flowers, birds, the wind and the rain.

A few years ago we put up Purple Martin houses and several seed feeders for the woodpeckers and songbirds. What a delight it has been. The martins are one of a few species of birds that live in colonies, and every year they migrate from South America to nest and raise their young. I am amazed at the comings and goings of our feathered friends. From establishing territory, mating, and building their nests, to feeding their young; it is truly an incredible source of wonderment and beauty.

Fly Anyway

I've experienced a lot of pain, and heartbreak in a short time. I've lost my beloved pet companion, my dad, and my husband has recently passed. Many times I didn't think there was much hope for joy ever again. But my Purple Martins have helped me find again, and keep hope through this tough time. These beautiful creatures fly thousands of miles to my backyard, build their nest, and raise their young all before summer's end. They encounter all sorts of perils to make their journey, but they fly anyway in hopes of raising their brood. As their hatchlings grow they tirelessly toil to feed each one to ensure their growth and strength to make their long journey back home to South America. Watching them has helped me keep going too. No matter the challenges, no matter the effort, I know I can make it through too.— Edna

The road ahead may be steep and rocky, with plenty of places to stumble...but let's not overlook the beauty that surrounds us, and the places to put our footing every step of the way.

Since as far back as I can remember, I have always found it fascinating how trees look dead in the winter. Consider the cherry blossom. It blooms delicate pink flowers in early spring, soon afterward, the flowers fall and leaves take their place. When the weather turns cold and temperatures drop, so do the leaves. Soon, this vibrant blooming tree is naked and devoid of its external beauty. The seasons change again, and the blooms return, often fuller and more vibrant, the leaves come back, and the tree is bigger and stronger than the year before. When the seasons change, it inherently does what it needs to do for survival. Even during a drought, a tree will conserve its nutrients to ensure the root system stays alive. It allows the outermost parts, such as the leaves, to be dropped, and in more favorable weather they return.

There is a lot we can learn from the tree. The winds blow and the storms move in, and this is when we need to reach deep inside. You may temporarily lose your leaves—happiness, joy, peace, security, confidence, but like the tree's deep roots, your inner strength is what gives you hope that your leaves will bud, blooms will blossom, and your fruit will thrive again. Keep hope, like the tree, and when the seasons change—and they will—you will be stronger and flourish again.

Character cannot be developed in ease and quiet. Only through experience of trial and suffering can the soul be strengthened, ambition inspired, and success achieved.—Helen Keller

Springtime in Oklahoma is beautiful, despite what you may hear about the tornadoes, it's a time to anticipate and appreciate the hope of new life. I look forward to seeing redbud trees bloom and the flowers blossom. In our own garden, I wait to see if the bulbs I planted survived and how many "volunteers" come back. Volunteers being the flowers that pop up here and there and sprout from flowers that are only supposed to bloom one season and never come back, yet some  manage to make it through the cold, icy winters and bring forth beauty once again.

I clean out old stalks and stems, and plant new flowers with fresh mulch to prepare for another growing season. I water them regularly and try to keep our four-legged kids from trampling them. I pull the weeds and provide them the perfect places to grow. By late summer, there are times I get too busy, and I fail to tend to my garden like I should. Somewhere along the line, I've lost sight of the beauty and purpose I have before me. The big baskets of blooms are barely hanging on to their skinny stems; the flowers in the beds aren't doing much better. Just to keep them watered in the very hot and dry summer is a twice-daily chore.

It just gets to be too much work; too much work because I let it get that way. Yet when I give the flowers a few minutes of my time daily, it's not a chore, but an opportunity. It's this little bit of nurturing for them, and for me, that will keep them beautiful and thriving. It's the same with our thoughts. A few minutes every day spent tending to our mind will keep our thoughts beautiful. Small efforts consistently and faithfully will come together, and before we realize it, it's no longer such an effort, but a natural response, and we feel and experience purpose and joy again.

Interesting note about the volunteers, they seem to survive through the toughest circumstances. They don't let the weeds smother them out or the months without water kill their will to survive. They also seem to grow in places they aren't supposed to. In the concrete crevice between our patio and house, behind the air conditioning unit, within the cracks in the sidewalk, there they bloom and thrive. No one has ever told them they shouldn't or couldn't, so they follow their inherent nature to put forth beauty anyway. So should we.

Gardening is not only therapeutic because of the intrinsic nature of it, but physiologically it is proven to lower the cortisol in our brain, which helps to reduce stress. Even getting our hands dirty from the soil in our garden can increase serotonin levels. According to research there is a specific soil bacteria, *Mycobacterium vaccae*, that triggers the release of serotonin. And with gardening, planting a seed or a little sprout and seeing it grow will activate the reward system in our brain and help to release endorphins that promote positive emotions and enhance our well-being (University of Bristol, 2007).

Gardening is purely a wonderful way to spend time in and with nature. We can enjoy it, and elevate our mood even from something small; a houseplant, a hanging basket, a bucket of cherry tomatoes, or a container of peppermint, lavender or sage. When life events and circumstances happen that we don't have control over, gardening is something literally at our fingertips that can help give us a feeling of purpose. Being responsible for life and growth gives us a sense of belonging and being needed. Putting our hands and our hearts into something other than our problems can provide a few moments to regain a sense of control, and a purpose that helps us take yet another step toward hope and happiness. Gardening is a beautiful way to restore our thoughts, a way to give new life to an old way of thinking.

The glory of gardening: hands in the dirt, head in the sun, heart with nature. To nurture a garden is to feed not just on the body, but the soul.—Alfred Austin

Joys come from simple
and
Natural things,

Mists over meadows, sunlight on
leaves,

The path of the moon over water.
Even rain and wind

and stormy clouds bring joy,

Just as knowing animals
and
Flowers
where they
live.

—Sigurd
F. Olson

©John Bindon Art

$\mathcal{W}$e need to find God, and He cannot be found in noise and restlessness. God is the friend of silence. See how nature - trees, flowers, grass- grows in silence; see the stars, the moon and the sun, how they move in silence...We need silence to be able to touch souls.—Mother Teresa

Scent

When Mom was confined to her bed, I would frequently bring flowers for her bedside table. I encouraged her, when she was really hurting or especially down, to close her eyes, then slowly and deeply breathe in the fragrance. It's a moment or two of something pleasurable in the midst of pain and anguish.

I do this often when our honeysuckle bush or our black locust tree is in full bloom. There is nothing more alive and invigorating, yet calming at the same time, than infusing our senses with the pure fragrance of fresh flowers or the scent of trees. Studies show as little as five minutes amongst the trees can improve both our physical and mental health. Trees and other forest vegetation emit a substance called phytoncides, this is linked to lowering stress, promoting positive feelings and improving concentration. The intricacies involved in how our brain interprets scents are quite amazing.

Just as music, exercise, prayer, and yoga trigger endorphins and the happy hormones, so does scent.

Fresh flowers, a pine forest, and lavender farms aren't always available to provide their natural fragrance; and since most of us don't have the ocean or forest outside our back door, we have to be creative and substitute when the real thing isn't available. Discovering how to use scents to our benefit is yet another color on the palette of emotional well-being.

Two of the gifts the three wise men bestowed upon baby Jesus were frankincense and myrrh—right next to gold. This makes me think these scents are quite valuable! Frankincense is believed to provide aid for an array of both physical and mental conditions. Myrrh is shown to contain up to 75 percent sesquiterpenes, which are compounds that can affect certain parts of your brain controlling your emotions and that produce many important endorphins and hormones in your body. They also have potential to treat heart disease and cancer *(IJMS, 2013)*. Smelling something beautiful can provide a sense of peace and calmness. Coupling this with other methods of relaxation can offer great benefits to how you feel. To get the most from these oils, they can be used in a diffuser,

or apply a diluted drop to your temples, base of your neck or chest, or add a few drops in your bath.

Burning *frankincense* or diffusing its oil helps eliminate feelings of depression and anxiety. You can also try rubbing a diluted drop on your temples or on your heart area. *Peppermint* oils are known to relieve mental fatigue, enhance alertness, and enhance memory. Peppermint will also add pep to your step and help get you going, or keep you going throughout the day. The uplifting aroma of *lemon* has been known to reduce stress and depression.

The essential oil of *eucalyptus* is widely recognized for opening the sinuses; however, it is also used to relieve headaches and mental fatigue.

Lavender is almost certainly the most widely used essential oil. Lavender is uplifting and relaxing. It is especially good for your bath, and a few drops placed near your pillow will help promote restful sleep. You can even rub a diluted drop on the back of your neck or on your temples. It is believed that lavender and vanilla together may activate the release of serotonin. *Jasmine* is used to help stimulate the stress-fighting hormones. It is thought to act as an antidepressant and relieve tension. Jasmine can also help you maintain quality sleep.

Sandalwood is often used to calm the nerves and promote relaxation. The scent of *Cedar* aids in reducing tension. *Vanilla* scents are used for relaxation. Vanilla is also used to help people stay calm during CAT scans and similar medical tests where calmness and restfulness are required.

Rosemary, orange, lemon, and grapefruit are all good mood enhancers. They are uplifting and promote cheerfulness. A few other oils specifically beneficial for improving mood and overall well-being are: cardamom, chamomile, and geranium. However, aside from the potential physiological responses, it just feels good to smell something pleasant, pure and beautiful.

We are surrounded by the splendor and awe of our Mother Earth. Beauty in nature is found everywhere; we only need to take the time to see it, to feel it, and to experience it. It is in the flowers growing around an office building or corner streetlight. It can be found in the birds on a high wire, the ridges on a leaf, or the texture of a tree trunk. Even the tiny ants swarming the cookie someone left on the patio table. How amazing that such tiny little creatures can work together and move an object so many times their weight.

A deeper exploration in finding beauty and joy in all of nature will do a hurting heart wonders. A hike, or a walk, just being outside in the cold, heat, rain or wind will get you in touch with your senses. Consider the different fauna and flora in your own community—get your hands in the dirt, face in the sun, and spirit surrounded with nature, you might just pick up a rock and find the face of hope looking back.

"*Lift up a rock, you will find Me there.*"
—Gospel of Thomas 77b

The Oak Tree

A mighty wind blew night and day.
It stole the Oak Tree's leaves away.
Then snapped its boughs
and pulled its bark
until the Oak was tired and stark.
But still the Oak Tree held its ground
while other trees fell all around.
The weary wind gave up and spoke,
"How can you still be standing Oak?"
The Oak Tree said, I know that you
can break each branch of mine in two,
carry every leaf away, shake my
limbs and make me sway.
But I have roots stretched in the earth,
growing stronger since my birth.
You'll never touch them, for you see
they are the deepest part of me.
Until today, I wasn't sure
of just how much I could endure.
But now I've found with thanks to you,
I'm stronger than I ever knew.

—Johnny Ray Ryder

Touching Hope

Love bears all things, believes all things, hopes all things, endures all things.—1 Corinthians 13:7

Soon after Mama died, I was afraid I would forget her voice, her face, her touch. These are things I feared would fade as the years went by. I still long for her presence, but the emptiness of losing her is less intense. I haven't forgotten her face or her voice; I just still miss them so very much. It's her touch, her hugs that seem the farthest away. I reminisce with photo albums or laugh and cry with old video tapes, which bring close to heart her beautiful smile and her warm voice. But if only I could hug her again.

Physical touch is essential for our well-being. Beginning at birth the need for touch is a critical element for both emotional and physical health, and remains so throughout our lifetime. Aside from the fact it just feels good to be hugged, there are a myriad of studies examining the effects of physical touch. The most telling discovery was that of the hormone oxytocin, often referred to as the "cuddle hormone," as it is released during close physical touch.

Many of us are familiar with the hormones serotonin and dopamine, but oxytocin is another hormone that gives us a sense of well-being and security. It helps with depression, lessens social anxiety and helps build trust in relationships.

We've probably all heard an apple a day will keep the doctor away, but a hug a day will help keep hopelessness away. Hug your children, your spouse, and your pets. Hold hands, squeeze a hand, and touch a shoulder. Offer a kind, friendly touch to friends and family; you will feel better, and so will they. This is especially crucial when there are relationship difficulties with a spouse, partner, or child. The release of oxytocin helps build connectedness, feelings of security, and trust—the foundation of all relationships.

One of the most uplifting touching is time with our pets. For me, time with our dogs can lift me from the lowest to the highest in only a moment. There is significant therapeutic value in spending quality time with our pets; the emotional reward is immediately evident, but the physiological benefits are immense as well.

Dogs and other furry animals are often used in therapeutic settings to help people and patients deal with a variety of conditions from cancer, depression, post-traumatic stress to anxiety, and so much more. However research goes beyond human touch and pet touch for oxytocin production. Some studies support the notion that holding and touching a soft teddy bear can promote the release of oxytocin, as well as enhance feelings of acceptance and generosity.

A group of researchers at the National University of Singapore decided to see if the touching of an inanimate object could do the same (Tai, Xue Zheng, and Narayanan, 2011). They separated their subjects into groups of four and asked them to pick two of the other three to work with. Participants were either told that everyone had picked them or that no one had picked them to be their partner. Later, each of the individuals were asked to rate a consumer product—a teddy bear. Half of them were asked to hold the bear while evaluating it as opposed to just viewing the bear. Among the subjects who were told that no one had picked them, those who touched the bear expressed more positive emotions at the end of the experiment than those who did not hold the teddy bear, although each of the subjects thought they had been rejected by their peers.

Simply put, the rejected people who touched the teddy bears felt better than those who didn't touch the bear. Those same people expressed positive emotions as often as the participants who were chosen. To sum it up, touching the teddy bear consistently made people feel better.

This study brought back memories of when I was child and always being the last one picked in team games. The dreadful wait in line hoping the captain would call my name—but who wants a girl without an arm to play soft ball or dodge ball? Who would have thought, a teddy bear would have made me feel better.

There is a reason why teddy bears can promote a sense of happiness or comfort. Our psyche has attached teddy bears to when our lives were simpler and carefree. Author and psychologist Corrine Sweet says, "It evokes a sense of peace, security, and comfort; it's human nature to crave these feelings from childhood to adult life" (Llorens, 2012).

A Friend

I saw the most warm and beautiful sight when I was getting my second round of chemo. I was sitting in the chair where I waited for the IV bag to empty into my arm. This would take about a half hour or more, so I sat there and forced positive thoughts to overcome the fearful ones, I prayed, and hoped this would be the last time. I looked across the large room and saw many others hoping the same as I was. What I saw when I looked to the left of me, was a woman who had reclined her chair all the way back with her eyes closed like she was sleeping. But what really grabbed me was the soft, fluffy, teddy bear that was on her chest; his furry, brown head nestled under her chin, her arms wrapped around his body, snuggling. She was holding her comfort, a friend who kept her company while she got her treatment. What a wonderful idea! Someone to be there while you go through the scariest time of your life. She seemed so satisfied and content with her bear. Whether it be sickness, insomnia, or any other uncomfortable difficult time, I now have my own teddy bear for comfort and confidence in the future. Just touching it helps calm my nerves.—Jana

Barren to Bears

After four years of marriage, Marc and I decided it was time to start our family—we wanted a baby. Truth is we didn't have much say over this after all. We tried to conceive for almost a year with no pregnancy; with each month only compounding one frustration after another.

During this time, Mama's health continued to fail, and I was learning to accept that not only would she never be the same, but Mama was dying. I knew I wouldn't be the same either. Mama knew how much I longed to have a baby, and I wanted so much, to be able to tell Mama that *her* baby—was going to have a baby.

Wednesday, December 27, 1995

> *Mom's excited that little Bambi (her Chihuahua) is pregnant, Bambi and I both were lying down with Mom, my head on her chest, Mom says "My babies are going to have babies." Marc and I just had another intrauterine insemination on Friday. We are hopeful we will conceive. Mom wants me to be pregnant—she said she wants to be able to hold my baby. I want her to hold my baby too.*

After several months of trying on our own, we pursued conception more aggressively with a fertility specialist and advanced treatments. In the beginning, it was charting my daily temperature, tracking my cycle, and oral fertility drugs. After three months, we advanced to fertility drugs by injection, weekly ultrasounds, and monthly intrauterine insemination at the clinic. Twelve to fourteen days later, the monthly lament began again. We went through several cycles, all to no avail. Since we could not afford in-vitro fertilization, this was our only hope for a pregnancy, and it seemed futile.

So why couldn't we conceive? After a slew of tests and ultrasounds, we concluded that not only could I not get pregnant; even if I could I would not be able to sustain a pregnancy. But *why?* I considered how a fourteen-year-old child could get pregnant or another baby could be aborted, abused or abandoned. There's that search for a reason again. I understand there isn't a blanket statement that can be made with regard to why so and so can get pregnant and I can't. It is the same with trying to understand why someone's spouse or child was killed in a car accident, while the drunk driver who caused the wreck walked away without a scratch. These are life events, and I have to choose how I'm going to respond them.

I don't know why Mama suffered and died so young, why I was born with one hand, or why I couldn't get pregnant. Instead of being bitter, jealous, or dwell on the *why*, I ask myself, the *how*—how can I give this life event or situation purpose? I have one good hand, so how can I use it for good?

We eventually accepted the realization that maybe it wasn't meant to be, however the hope that a baby would still come naturally remained in my heart. It matters not that it never came to fruition, it matters how I choose to cope with our loss; the loss of a life, a future we thought we would have with a child.

Sunday, January 6, 1996

When I talked to Mom this evening she was sad, she told me to tell Marc to give me love and tenderness. Yesterday we found out I'm not pregnant. When I saw her earlier she asked, "Did Marc hold you and hug you a long time?" I answered, "Yes he did."

*L*ater that same summer, we found a little dog wandering around in our neighborhood. He was a tattered matted mess from neglect and time on the street, yet his spirit remained so gentle, and so—happy. We loved on him, fed him and gave him shelter for the night, knowing we'd need to find him a home. The following day we took him to a groomer and a veterinarian for an exam and to treat the sores that covered his body; when we picked him up we could barely recognize him, there before our eyes stood a little miniature schnauzer. Needless to say, we found him a home— ours. We named him Frisco.

Late one evening a short time after Mama died, I was holding Frisco in my arms. He was so comfortably sprawled out in my lap, trusting me and letting me love him. I gazed at him and whispered my thoughts out loud, "You're my little baby." It was at that moment that I realized maybe God had answered my prayer; He had given me my little baby. A scraggly little schnauzer wasn't the baby I was hoping for, but since that moment, Frisco has forever been my baby.

Four years later, Frisco acquired a horrific autoimmune disease. After two blood transfusions and ten days in the hospital, Frisco's life was over. Frisco wasn't just a dog or pet; he was our family, he was my baby. He came to me at a time I really needed him; Mama was dying and I wasn't able to conceive. But this tore an even deeper hole in our hearts. When Frisco died, I had recently discovered the world of making teddy bears. I was working on one particular little bear; however I was so sick with grief, I didn't think I could make another stitch. I was not only grieving the death of Frisco, but it reopened the deep pain of losing my mama and the loss of the child I never had. Through eyes filled with tears and a broken heart, I finished that bear, and I found hope in her tender comfort. I named her Blue, she was just what I needed; I was broken, yet somehow, she comforted me. It was a teddy bear that gave me comfort—and hope. And comfort and hope would be what I needed the next few months.

After Frisco died, we adopted another little dog to help us through our grief, a six-month-old miniature schnauzer we named Mako. Six weeks after Frisco's death, Mako died from complications after being neutered. Eight weeks after Mako died, Marc and I separated and subsequently divorced. The death of our dogs opened a doorway to our pain and loneliness, and shed light on how emotionally drained and distant we had become.

It was then I was able to channel my grief through creating, bringing life to pieces of material and fabrics. I wasn't ever able to make a baby, but I could sure make some teddy bears.

Blue

*Hope is being able to see that there is
Light despite all of the darkness.
—Desmond Tutu*

*J*n this sad world of ours, sorrow comes to all; and, to the young, it comes with bitterest agony, because it takes them unawares. The older have learned to ever expect it. J am anxious to afford some alleviation of your present distress. Perfect relief is not possible, except with time. You cannot now realize that you will ever feel better. Js not this so? And yet it is a mistake. You are sure to be happy again. To know this, which is certainly true, will make you some less miserable now. J have had experience enough to know what J say; and you need only to believe it, to feel better at once. —Abraham Lincoln

Jackson's Gift

In 2007, Jennifer's eight-month-old baby boy died from sudden infant death syndrome. Jennifer honors her son Jackson with a website she created in his memory to help others who have lost a loved one. The Center for Help and Hope, a nonprofit organization dedicated to people who are hurting and are in need of hope.

Jennifer shares these heartfelt yet comforting words surrounding the time of her loss:

> *Nighttime is frequently the most difficult time. It can be an indeterminably long time between sunset and sunrise. A small thing that helped me in a huge way was to hold on to a teddy bear at night. I slept with a teddy bear for many months. And it helped. I needed something to hold onto. I needed something to hug and hold. It wasn't my baby but it was a lot better than nothing. And it did give me quite a bit of comfort. Sometimes I still sleep with that teddy bear, seven years later. But don't be discouraged by the fact that I still grieve and cry and hug a teddy bear seven years after my son died. You'll never "get over it." You'll never forget your baby. You will always miss your baby. The good news is, the pain will, over time, go from being continuous to being occasional. It will still be extremely intense at times but those times will happen a lot less often. You will be able to feel happiness again. It's very important to know that.*

She offers the following words of wisdom to family and friends:

> *Honor your pain. My pain is a testament to the fact that my son was loved. It says his life mattered. It will not always hurt this bad. Yes, it will always hurt and yes you will always miss your child, but the pain will not always be this intense. Life will be good again someday.*

No More Empty Arms

After years of trying to get pregnant, it finally happened. In the fall of 2009, my wife Cindy suspected she might be expecting. Without my knowledge, early one morning she took a home pregnancy test. It came back positive. After so many years of failure, my wife was beside herself with joy. Yet amazingly, she was able to keep the results a secret from me throughout the day.

That evening, when I walked into our kitchen for dinner, I saw a box sitting where my place-setting usually is. "What's this?" I asked. "It's a gift for you." "Can I open it before dinner?" "Sure" she responded coolly. I opened the box, and saw a note attached to a "positive" pregnancy test, which said, "God has answered our prayers." Underneath the note was bib that said "I love my Daddy." "I suppose a scene like that is played out by couples every day, in their own special way.

Like them, we were now on the pregnancy pathway. Regular doctor visits, ultrasounds, and making a million plans for the arrival of our baby. When week twenty came around, like most expecting parents, we were excited to finally have the ultrasound, which would tell us what gender our baby would be. The ultrasound began with the technician sizing the baby while chatting casually with us. A few moments later, she gave us the information we had been excitedly waiting for. In a halting, distracted voice, she said, "This... baby... is... going... to... be.... a... girl!" We were so excited. We both had a sense we were having a girl, but to have this confirmed was an amazing moment. We had already decided we would name her Reagan Marie. After giving us this great news, the technician continued her work, but she became more subdued. As the minutes went on, she became less engaged in speaking with us and increasingly focused on her screen.

She asked us several unusual questions, a few of which she repeated. "How far along are you?" "What is your due date?" "How sure are you of your conception date?"

She went on to tell us she saw some things that were "unusual," but not necessarily bad news. As a precaution, she wanted us to see a perinatologist. We scheduled an appointment for the next day. Neither of us sensed any significant alarm, so I went ahead with a previously scheduled trip to Florida.

When Cindy met with the perinatologist, he carefully reviewed the ultrasound data. He then gave her the news that would change our lives. He said our child almost certainly had Trisomy 18. Trisomy 18 is a genetic disorder that, in clinical terms, is "incompatible with life." Most Trisomy 18 babies do not make it to term. Those that do usually live minutes, perhaps hours, in rare cases they live days. From that point forward, we were counseled by multiple doctors to abort the pregnancy. We never gave the idea serious consideration, being convinced that all life is a gift from God. We loved our daughter immensely, and were going to walk this journey with her every day God would give us with her. In utero, we treated Reagan Marie like any other baby. We talked to her, prayed for her, giggled at her movements, and enjoyed her growth.

Somehow we knew she was happy, and we were happy with her. About 1am, on May 4, 2010, Cindy was awakened by a strange sensation. Her water had broken. Reagan was at thirty weeks. We did not know what to expect, but we were concerned. At the hospital, Cindy's labor progressed throughout the morning. At 10:03 AM, Reagan was born.

Like most parents, we could not believe she finally had arrived. We could not stop looking at her. We talked to her, stroked her head, and told her how beautiful she was. We were determined to just enjoy her for as long as we had her. We did not know how long that would be. The doctor thought perhaps eight hours, but nobody really knew. Reagan barely moved after she was born. Around 10:20 AM, Cindy suddenly had a sensation that Jesus was standing next to her bed. He was smiling, and his arms were open wide. A few minutes later, a nurse pressed a stethoscope to Reagan's little chest. She announced, "I am not getting a heartbeat." The time was 10:24 AM. Our little girl had left us.

We spent the rest of the day holding her as family and close friends came to visit us in the hospital. We hugged and cried with them as we remembered our little girl's brief life. We cherished every minute we had with her. As the day progressed, day changed into night, and then night became late night. It was time to say goodbye to Reagan Marie—for now. Later that evening, in an emotionally charged moment, we passed Reagan's little body to two solemn men from a local funeral home.

Before our trip to the hospital, like most expectant parents, we had pre-packed our bags. One item we brought to the hospital that most parents don't was a teddy bear. Cindy had read that a mom who was at high risk of perinatal loss could take great comfort in holding on to a teddy bear when she no longer had a baby in her arms. After Reagan's body left us in the hospital, Cindy held onto the teddy bear. We both cried, and began the mourning process that would intensify in the days and months to come. But that teddy bear, in a small and simple way, brought some comfort to Cindy. At one point the bear lay next to Reagan and touched her. So in a way, the bear carried with it some sense of Reagan's presence and memory. In May 2011 Reagan Marie's family alongside with Northside Hospital established the Reagan Marie Teddy Bear Fund. The hope of the fund is to provide moms who have experienced perinatal loss with a teddy bear to hold on to. No teddy bear can replace a child. However, a teddy bear can bring some meaning and comfort into a situation that is otherwise filled with pain and sorrow. The Reagan Marie Teddy Bear Fund's mission is simple: no mom should ever again leave the hospital with empty arms. Every mom who experiences a perinatal loss will be given a teddy bear with a note of encouragement attached. –The Baima Family

Molly Christine

We lost our angel, Molly Christine, at thirty-four weeks, on May 30, 2010. I had not felt our active girl all day on the 29th. That night I went to the hospital to get checked and make sure Molly was all right. We were told that our precious daughter no longer had a heartbeat. She died from a tight true knot in her cord. Devastated would not even begin to describe how we felt. I was given a weighted teddy bear from a dear friend from high school. This bear weighed three pounds. In an effort to have a bear that weighed the same as Molly, I bought a shell and a package of rice. In the middle of the produce aisle, I carefully weighed rice, fluff, and the shell. I am sure people thought I was crazy, but I did not care. I went home and with my children and husband, we created the very first Molly Bear.

For the first time in weeks, I was able to sleep holding her. It was then that I knew I had to find a way to help other angel families.

I started making these bears for other angel mommies that I had become close to in several support groups. I had committed to one bear per paycheck and soon I had requests and a desire to make more. I went to my sister Amanda and I was venting about what I wanted and that I wasn't sure how to make it happen. In a few hours she called me back with a plan, and within a week we jumped in feet first.

Since then, Bridget and her team of volunteers have provided thousands of weighted bears to empty arms in all fifty states and twenty-four countries. What more beautiful way to give meaning to your own loss than by helping others who are hurting from the same type of loss. If you know anyone in need or would like to contribute to their cause, you can reach them at *www.mollybears.com.*

The more one forgets himself by giving himself to a cause to serve, or another person to love, the more human he is. —Viktor Frankl

Give every day the chance to become the most beautiful day of your life.—Mark Twain

Teddy Bear Tales

A teddy bear you can share, but more than a bear, it's showing someone you care.

One rainy day in 2004, I was exhibiting some of my handmade bears at a local art festival. It was outdoors, and it had been raining heavily all weekend. Although the event was held under tents, it was still dreadful. Nonetheless, I had many teddy bears displayed cheerfully on my table. Despite the weather, a lot of people were still out browsing the treasures of local artists.

I remember watching a woman walking up the aisle, her face appeared downcast. I wondered if it was the weather, or maybe she had personal strife that brought her spirit down. I watched her look at one table, then turn and browse another table, with her demeanor unchanging. At the moment her eyes connected with the bears on my table, her face instantly lit up. The look of despair I saw earlier had changed to joy. I will never forget this transformation. I knew then I was making teddy bears for a purpose.

Whatever it was that had her spirits down was absolutely erased the moment she saw the bears. She picked each one up while smiling and giggling. When she finally walked away from my table, the weather was still dreary and she still had her problems, but I do know her spirit was lifted, even if only for those moments. I know the bears helped comfort her on a rainy day and made her a day a bit brighter.

Teddy bears connect with the heart and

just seem to know if we need to be cheered up, encouraged, or just need a quiet, comforting companion. When people are hurting, we sometimes struggle with the right words to say. A sweet teddy bear says all the right things without saying a word. A teddy bear can speak from the heart of the giver to the heart of the receiver by just being there. The teddy bear can be there when you are not. It represents you and your love.

Sometimes, it's just the struggles we encounter in our daily life—rejection, illness, losing a job, relationship difficulties—a teddy bear might be just what you—or someone—needs to lift the spirit. We grow up and begin to think we no longer need the comforts and securities we may have had as a child. The fact is, most of us still have that part of us dwelling within. During lonely or difficult times, our insecurities come

to the surface. Just maybe what comforted us as a child can comfort us now.

Teddy bears transcend time. Young or old, male or female, a teddy bear is universal, and so is what it represents—love. Love reaches to all corners of the world, and so does a teddy bear. Love is truly expressed without words, and so it is with a teddy bear. The bearer can experience feelings of comfort, of acceptance, of remembrance, of joy, and of love. It is a reminder that the person who gave the teddy bear cares. It is a reminder of innocence, of a more hopeful time. A teddy bear is a tangible representation of so many things that we often have difficulty expressing or sharing.

A teddy bear is a way of sharing memories, sharing joy, sharing a hug, and sharing love. When we don't have the right words to say, a teddy bear is a beautiful, collective way to say so many things without saying a word. It means I love you, I miss you, I'm happy for you, I'm sorry, or simply I care about you. We all need comfort and compassion at some time in our lives, and giving or receiving a teddy bear might just help get us through those times. So the next time your down or lonely, try squeezing or holding a teddy bear. And if you know someone going through a difficult time, give them a teddy bear. They really are the most perfect gift you can give—or receive.

Throughout my work and while collecting stories for *Bear with Hope,* I met people with unique experiences and stories of how a teddy bear helped see them through some of the most difficult and painful times in their life. I also stumbled upon some interesting tidbits about teddy bears as well as some remarkable accounts of a teddy bear being a token reminder of hope. I'd like to share these heartwarming stories with you here. I hope you can glean some encouragement and inspiration from these diverse and special situations.

The Teddy Bear on My Bed

There's a teddy bear that sits on my bed. At forty-six years old, it's probably not apropos, but regardless, it is there. It is there to serve as a reminder for me. A reminder of love. When I was going through an extremely painful time in my life, I took my youngest son Matthew to a local summer festival. It was a warm June evening, and Matthew was twelve at the time. The streets were crowded with people. Families, teenagers, and children were scrambling to ride every ride. The smell of cotton candy and fresh popped popcorn filled the air. Crowds gathered to hear local bands, buy hotdogs and soda, and enjoy the fresh warm air of early summer in the Midwest. All in all, it was a perfect summer evening. But all I saw that night were couples. Couples in love. Men with their arms wrapped around their women, sharing a bite to eat, holding hands as they listened to the music play. More couples waiting in line to ride the Ferris wheel, or the tilt a whirl.

And seeing those couples so happy and in love brought an even greater loneliness to my heart. It was all I could do not to cry. I swallowed back the tears, hoping that Matthew was enjoying himself enough to be oblivious to my pain. I felt cheated that evening. Cheated out of love. Cheated out of the security and comfort that being in a relationship brought. Cheated out of having the life I had always dreamed about. Cheated out of having a wonderful husband and father for my children. And I felt so very alone. "Snap out of it Debbie! Stop feeling sorry for yourself!" my inner voice kept telling me. But when your heart is breaking, there is no rationalizing with it. It must feel the pain. It must mourn the loss before it can heal.

There were of course that night, many carnival games to play. Weathered gents calling out for us to knock down the bottles and win a prize, pick out the right rubber ducky with the lucky marking on its belly, and so on. I had never really enjoyed spending money on trying to win a cheaply sewn stuffed animal, but Matthew was persistent, begging for a chance to win a prize. "Please Mom," he begged. "I know I can do it! Let me try!" "Fine Matthew," I said. "Knock yourself out!" Anything to keep him happy and get through this evening. The first attempt brought us only a loss of the dollar I had spent "One more time Mom, please!" Matthew begged. "Wouldn't you rather go on a ride?" I asked. "No Mom, please. I know I can do it this time!" Another dollar spent. Another dollar lost. "OK, Matthew, enough. Let's move on." Once more Matthew begged to try. Please! I just know this time I will win. I promise! Just one more try. Please, Mom!" Already feeling low, I relented and gave him the money.

And just like he promised, this time, Matthew won. The pride glowed in my son's eyes as he picked out just the right prize. And just and I was ready to walk away from that little booth, Matthew turned to me and presented me with the most beautiful yellow teddy bear that I had ever seen. I looked up to see such a pure beautiful love reflected in his eyes, that I could not help but cry and hold him and the teddy bear close to my heart. Matthew knew all along how sad and lonely I had been feeling. And in his twelve-year-old heart, he wanted to ease my pain in whatever way he could.

From that day on until the day I die, that beautiful soft yellow teddy bear will always hold a special place in my life. It will always represent to me the beauty of true love. We often forget, at least I do, that love surrounds us each and every day. We search for a particular kind of love, one that we feel we are missing out on, only to miss out on the real love that is right in front of us. The love of our children. The love of a friend. The love of a

sibling or a parent. So that teddy bear that sits on my bed, that I look at each and every morning, is my reminder every single day, to be thankful for the love that is in my life. I know now what real love is all about. It is present each and every day. If only we are aware enough to see it.

And yes, I still would like to have that special someone to share the rest of my life with. I know that I will meet him when the time is right. But right now, right this very moment, I have five very special someone's to share my life with. I am blessed. And I am loved. And I am grateful for that. Each and every day.—Debbie

Good Bears of the World is one of many nonprofit organizations that provide thousands of teddy bears each year to comfort the hurting. Families and individuals in need include victims of devastating and catastrophic weather events, domestic violence, tragedies through fire, and accidents. The teddy bears are a gesture, a token reminding them that someone cares that might just help ease the grief and suffering in the hearts and homes of our communities.

Good Bears are also given to the sick, injured, and underprivileged children as well as lonely seniors and veterans in hospitals. Firefighters, police officers, emergency workers, psychologists, and grief counselors have discovered the teddy bear's special healing power for both children and adults in therapy or traumatic situations. Sometimes the pain and sadness are so great, the grieving need embrace another and see a compassionate and understanding face. For others, it is just to provide a simple and sweet companion during a lonely time in their lives.

My Cop Bear

At five years of age I was the youngest child of three. One day we were coming home from a family trip in Tulsa, Oklahoma. We were on the Turner Turnpike toward Oklahoma City when my dad lost control of our family minivan. I remember flipping the first time, but after that I was knocked unconscious. The minivan tumbled end over end a total of four times. We landed upside down teetering on a guardrail.

Two semi trucks stopped to block the traffic and ran to our aid. One truck driver spoke to my mom and asked if they could pull the kids out, starting with the youngest. I was pulled from the wreckage and handed off to another truck driver. I remember being covered in glass. The truck driver proceeded to carefully remove the glass filled clothes and then covered me with his own shirt. I sat with this truck driver while they pulled the rest of my family from the van and treated my dad and sister in an ambulance.

Meanwhile, an Oklahoma State Trooper brings me a teddy bear from his car. The teddy had on a little red and white t-shirt that had the Oklahoma state trooper logo on it. This bear was named Cop Bear, I still have him, he will always be my memory of that scary day, but more, when a State Trooper gave me the best thumb sucking buddy ever.—Emma

My First Bear

I really never had teddy bears growing up, I'm a guy and really just didn't want them. I liked real boy toys...guns and cars and stuff. However, now many years later, I've had a lot of things going on that has been very hard to deal with. The stress and pain of being an adult has been tough and often keeps me awake all night. When I do sleep, it's nightmares and anxiety filled sleep. It's been this way for years and I didn't know what I needed or even what to do. So it happens one day in class, a professor was giving out teddy bears to the students that were there on time...surprisingly I was actually on time that day and got a teddy bear. When he handed me the teddy bear, the moment I touched my teddy bear, I was so overwhelmed with emotion I was afraid I was actually going to cry right there in class! Not good for a twenty-four-year-old tough guy! The touch of my teddy bear was an instant release of emotions; the loneliness and pain came flooding through but so did a feeling of hope. It allowed me to feel. So now when something is bringing me down, I just talk to my teddy bear, especially before bedtime. I can say anything to him, unlike the world around me who so often expects something, he does not. I can say anything on my mind, meaningful or not, good or bad or just plain stupid. And no I do not expect him to talk back, but just there listening to me without judgment, or without gossiping to others. A simple way to let out my frustrations and not take them to bed. I sleep much better nowadays.—James

Silent No More

My second husband had a serious drinking problem, was good-looking and clever; clever enough to never leave any bruises for family or friends to see. Myself, always wanting to please, and a woman with a mission, I thought I could fix him, instead, I just learned to tolerate the abuse. As time went on things got harder to handle. I began missing more work. I had my brother come and take my daughter to the safety and security of my parent's home. Soon after, I called my husband's work, and when his boss answered, he had asked me how I was doing. That being unusual, I asked about his concern for me. He shared with me that everyone thought I had a mental breakdown, crashed our truck into a tree, and they thought I was in the hospital. This was the story my husband had told them.

I sat for the rest of the day deciding how to escape, how to get away and to stay away. Not really understanding what I was feeling, too confused about making any decisions, I finally reached out to my mother for help. The early hours of the next morning, my father, brother, my best friend and her husband all came to take me home and away from the abusive situation I was in. I was so messed up in my head—I couldn't even tie my shoes. They all began packing up my stuff, while my father called the police to make sure my husband stayed away until we were gone. All I could do was hold my big teddy bear. I rode home in my friend's car, and just held tightly to my bear. It was a long silent drive home. But I had my bear; he was the one who was always there for me, who was there every time I needed someone. I held him in silence and cried. When we arrived home, my daughter met us— "please tell me we're never going back!" We never went back. As time went on, I recognized I had always looked for a man that I could fix, but I really needed to look inside and take care of me. And that's what I was finally able to do.

—Lisa

Lisa's story is all too common in domestic violence situations. But Lisa mustered her strength and she asked for help. She recognized she need not suffer in silence alone, and she chose to reach out for help. Lisa's bear was later given to her daughter; it provides comfort, but it also serves as a reminder of a time when Lisa found her voice and found hope again.

A Teddy Bear Smile

I am a twenty-six-year-old male who sleeps with a teddy bear. I was an only child so my teddy bear was with me through a lot. Occasionally I'll still tell my teddy how much I love him, although I don't need it to sleep, it sure helps on those nights when my insomnia kicks in.

My closest friends don't know about my teddy bear, and this is a fear of mine to be ridiculed over something I hold so dear to my heart. I only shared this secret with my girlfriends over the years and I have found in every relationship I've been in, it has shown the affectionate side of me when I surprise the girl with my teddy. Aside from my teddy bear, I am a pretty intimidating person to meet, and can give off an aura of not being a nice guy unless I get a good gut feeling about your personality, otherwise trust has to be earned.

Through my teenage years I was around drugs with certain family members, and this critical stage of self-development has affected who I am, seeing parents smoking in front of their children, seeing how skinny the kids are because they always fed their habit and not their children. I lost the ability to see the good that was there because I was so focused on hating the bad. When I was in junior high I separated myself from just about everyone and this is when I started to shut everyone out even my parents who always loved me. I was still a good student up until sophomore year when I got into the drugs. Life eventually became a stream of white noise that produced wretched headaches.

Being so young, why was I doing this to myself I asked my Teddy one morning, him staring back at me with his ever loving smile just made something in me snap and I cried from morning until night. The next morning, I quit cold turkey; I started focusing on all the positive and trying to figure out what to do with my life. I  *took an active role in my life for the good. I got back into athletics and eating right, socialized a little more and connected with my family again. I was on the road to being happy inside, and finally started maturing into a man.—Ben*

For Ben, his teddy bear served a greater purpose in that moment. It was Teddy's smile that ignited hope in Ben; but it was Ben that garnered strength to make the right choices to change his life. He reached out to family, involved himself in positive relationships and activities, and discovered a newfound hope in life.

A Window of Hope

I was engaged to a truly, wonderful human being. He was a good man, and we were in love, and simply happy. Then a car accident took his life and took him away from me. But he wasn't the only one who died that day, I died too. I tried for several months to get my head straight, but I wasn't able to pull myself out the darkness I had fallen into. I had to free myself of this pain. I was going to end my life I had been dying through anyway, because I certainly hadn't been living. I hurt so deep I thought it would never go away, so I was just going to make it go away. One day I decided to walk around the mall, something I used to love to do when I was a teenager. It wasn't the same, there was no joy. I was just taking in the last bits of pieces of my life. It was then as I turned the corner I saw a teddy bear in a store window. It was just hanging there on display. It seemed to be looking directly at me. I walked past it, but felt this draw to go back to it. I turned around and stood there and stared at it. Something switched inside me. It was as if the teddy bear was telling me to hang on. I couldn't do what I was going to do. This teddy bear had his eyes on mine and I just felt something different. I started crying. But it wasn't tears of despair, it was tears of relief. I knew I must push through it and things will get better again, I will get better. And I did. I looked closer at my life since Paul's death, and at the choices I was making, and realized it wasn't my fiancé's death that had me feeling such despair; it was the choices I was making since he died. It was how I quit caring for myself, how I withdrew from life, that's where my despair was coming from. I'm back involved with things I used to love to do, and have found new creative ways to express myself and enjoy life again. I am now filled with gratitude for the time I did have with my love. I am so thankful for that little teddy bear. It was just there, its face, its look, it was what I needed, I have a new love for teddy bears now, I also have a new life, one filled with hope.—Sandra

My Bear in Arms

I am a forty-six-year-old man who will never give up his pooh bear, because of what it reminds me of—a parent's love of their child on vacation and the memories of happy and sad times of a lifetime. When I was about five years old, my mom and dad took me and my brother to Disney World and I got my special bear. He has been with me ever since. I have had him at college, I took him with me when I deployed for missions in Iraq and Afghanistan, and he is here with me now in Amman Jordan.

First arrival in theater is very scary. Being shuffled into very stoic accommodations, usually late at night after long travel, with no immediate contact with family, friends, or any of the comforts of home is unsettling. And when the lights go out and you're all alone with the sounds of firefights and explosions in the distance fear can give way to dread and horror. Pooh was always a comfort to me beyond words. He was, and is, a physical reminder of the security my loving parents gave me as a child - that indescribable security that no matter what monsters are under my bed or hidden in my closet - I am safe.

He is a symbol of the stability of my life back in the States. He reminds me of the innocence of my childhood, and of how innocent my kids are. He keeps me grounded in loving the simple things in life. Every morning we get out of bed and we move him to the couch. Every night we turn out the lights, lock the doors and go to bed. And when I travel, he has that special pocket in my backpack. When we travel through the airports of the world he gets the warmest welcomes from the very youngest kids and the seniors alike. I have come across a lot of cynics and nay-sayers in the past 40+ years. "Oh, you need a teddy bear!" Well, I can say this. I played college and semi-pro football, I kick-boxed on the circuit for five years, I have survived two war zones and an emotionally difficult divorce. And through it all, I can still laugh and bring happiness to my work and personal life because I have my bear. He's lost an eye and his fur is a bit matted and worn, but I would not trade him for anything in the world. With him I know that I can laugh and it is okay to cry. I know I am safe even in the most dangerous times, and I know that no matter what, it will always work out. So yes, I need my Pooh bear.—Benjamin

It's a Plane, it's Birds, it's Teddy Bears?

Imagine walking along the street when you look to the clear blue sky and see a bunch of things falling from it. What on earth—or in the sky—could it be? As they come closer, you see it's—teddy bears? On July 4, 2012, that's exactly what happened in the small town of Ivyanets, Belarus. The teddy bear airdrop was a year in the making and chartered by two Swedes associated with Studio Total, a Swedish advertising agency.

The two pilots who led the effort stated they felt compelled to bring attention to the harshly suppressed people of Belarus; a country believed to be one of the last dictatorships in Europe. Despite the danger of being shot down, they took a small plane over the heavily guarded airspace of Belarus and airdropped over eight hundred parachuting teddy bears. Each of the teddy bears held cards and notes with pro-democracy and freedom of speech support.

One of the pilots involved in the teddy bear invasion acknowledged that the idea to use teddy bears came from Belarusian pro-democracy activists, who had been arrested on many occasions by the authorities. Other pro-rights activists started carrying teddy bears with protest slogans demanding freedom of speech. These activists were arrested, and the teddy bears confiscated by the government. The pilot stated that the airdrop was intended as a show of support— "We flew in teddy bears and airdropped them to support those arrested teddy bears."

We can only hope the people of Belarus understood the true meaning behind the bears. They are not suffering alone. When asked about the danger of the mission, he stated that every day, people risk their lives in activities just for fun or fortune; his belief was why not risk your life for something that has meaning and purpose.

Bearing it Through

In some way, suffering ceases to be suffering at the moment it finds a meaning, such as the meaning of a sacrifice.—Victor Frankl

The process of working through and beyond grief, no matter the cause of that grief, takes time. It is what we choose to do with this time—and what we do with our thoughts—which will determine how soon we find our hope and happiness again.

When we have a goal, such as to save money for a car or for vacation, we don't save it all at once; we discipline ourselves to save a set amount from each paycheck, and when possible, throw in a few extra dollars here and there. Before you know it, we have achieved our goal. Apply these same principles to changing your mind and your thought process. It takes commitment and perseverance, but you can have peace, experience joy, and be happy again. Doing just one thing, one time, such as meditating, music, exercise, or art, isn't going to make our pain disappear, but like hope, it helps us get through the difficult times and to a place where we can discover peace again. If we make a deliberate choice to actively restore our thoughts by taking these small steps—*we will feel better.*

It takes effort and commitment to make positive changes in our thoughts and in our life. Regrettably sometimes we get in a rut. I have, and perhaps you have too. Somehow we find ourselves comfortable being unhappy because it's easier than taking action to make meaningful changes in our life. It's like losing weight; I would venture to say that most of us know *how* to lose weight—eat less, eat healthy, and exercise. It's a pretty simple concept. However, it's the application of those principles that we find too hard or challenging. We must commit to our hope and happiness by adopting the right attitude, and it all starts with the thoughts in our mind.

We have at our threshold the ability to choose fun, thoughtful, relaxing, and healthy ways to provide nourishment for our spirit and emotional well-being. We have many options and creative ways to naturally produce healthy hormones and endorphins we need for emotional wellness, and at the same time reduce the stress and anxiety causing hormones. Too often we do nothing, or we turn to unnatural and unhealthy habits with isolation, alcohol, addiction, or over-medicating to numb our pain; but in reality, it numbs us from feeling that which we seek most—happiness and joy.

It is my hope that the pages in this book offer words of encouragement and hope. Whatever your situation is, I hope you know that you have an amazing ability inside you that is beyond human understanding.

At the beginning of the book, I said when life knocks the stuff out of us, we should pick it up, get some new, and stuff it back in. The old stuff is the struggles, sorrow, and strife we go through. The new stuff is the courage, the hope, the peace, and the strength we obtain with our commitment and perseverance.

You may wonder—why put the old stuff back in? However if not for the very experiences we endure, we would not otherwise achieve the fortitude of mind and heart. It is because of the pain, that we obtain the strength and spirit we now have. Only when we understand that joy and sorrow must co-exist will we experience life to the fullest.

The emptiness you feel from your grief is the same emptiness that will be filled with hope and happiness. Our experiences strengthen our spirit and give us a doorway to move forward in hope and faith in ourselves—and in the world in which we live. And if we allow it, our pain will serve a greater purpose even beyond ourselves.

There is no quick fix to move beyond challenging and hard times. A life event that has you down, depressed or discouraged is just that—a life event. It's not you, it's not me, we are only experiencing it. The amazing part is we can choose to respond to these events in a positive, hopeful, and more constructive way. Let us strive to be a giver of hope, joy, kindness, and gratitude. By doing so, we exponentially increase the value and meaning in own our life.

One stroke of the paintbrush did not create the magnificent ceiling in the Sistine Chapel, but one stroke after another, after another did. A spectacular diverse array of paints, colors, and techniques all came together to create this masterpiece. It is known that Michelangelo suffered extreme physical pain throughout this process. For nearly four years he contorted his body for hours on end to reach difficult places; an extended arm with paint dripping on his face all the while standing or laying on a wooden platform at extreme heights. He was in such physical agony, he even wrote a sonnet about his suffering. He also endured incredible emotional stress. It is recorded that he was conflicted about accepting the job and sorely regretted it; he thought of himself as a sculptor, not a painter, and feared this would ruin his reputation. But he persevered regardless of the obstacles, beliefs, and challenges. And now his paintings in the Sistine Chapel are considered the most iconic masterpieces in Italian Renaissance history. Goethe wrote, "Without having seen the Sistine Chapel, one can form no appreciable idea of what one man is capable of achieving."

So it is with your life, your commitment to be happy, and the restoration of your heart. It might take some unconventional means to restore your hope and happiness, but commit to it anyway. It is true, we do not know what we're capable of, and while we hope for it, we can't always see how the colors come together to create our own masterpiece—our life. Listen to beautiful music, pray, dance, create something, bake something, and gift something. Watch a funny movie or tell funny stories, and laugh until your belly hurts. Perhaps doing one thing is all you need to get moving forward, so make that first stroke of the brush, it will give you hope to help get you through the next hour, and sometimes, that's all we need to keep on.

By the same token, integrating multiple strategies of self-care through prayer, relaxation, gratitude, creativity, and giving will consistently restore your belief in yourself, the people around you, and how you approach your circumstances.

Learn to be active in your commitment to hope. Persevere through the challenges. Replace negative, harmful thoughts with positive thoughts, words, and actions. Restore your mind with beautiful, affirmative beliefs of peace, love, and hope, and you will find yourself in a good place.

I still miss my mama, I grieve, I cry, I wish she were here. On those days I want and need to feel close to her, I'll reach for the photo albums to see her big smile. If I am longing for her voice, I'll play an old VCR tape. But when I need to touch her again, I'll hold my teddy bear. Despite having only one hand, I found purpose for the one hand I did have. It took many struggles and deep loss to discover that purpose, but when Mama died, she left behind a life of love, perseverance, and hope; yet perhaps most importantly, the gift of faith—and, of course, that old fur coat.

Mama's Bear

I can do all things through Him who gives me strength.—Phil 4:13

The deeper that sorrow carves into your being, the more joy you can contain. Is not the cup that holds your wine the very cup that was burned in the potter's oven? And is not the lute that soothes your spirit, the very wood that was hollowed with knives? When you are joyous, look deep into your heart and you shall find it is only that which has given you sorrow that is giving you joy. When you are sorrowful look again in your heart, and you shall see that in truth you are weeping for that which has been your delight.—Khalil Gibran

Acknowledgements

To the beautiful people who gave permission, participated, or contributed to *Bear with Hope*. To each of you who shared your words of wisdom, art and creativity, or your personal stories, I thank you.

Additional recognition for photographs of original artwork

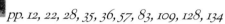 *pp. 12, 22, 28, 35, 36, 57, 83, 109, 128, 134*
Janet Kruskamp- *janetkruskamp.com*

pp. 40, 114, 117, 130, 138
John Bindon *www.mgllicensing.com*

Other soft sculpture teddy bear photographs courtesy of:

Michelle Lamb, *oneandonlybears.com* pp. 67, 82
Denise Purrington, *denisepurringtonbears.com* p. 87
Thea De Bruin, *millymedesigns.com* pp. 80, 82
Chantal Giroux, *chantalbears.jigsy.com* p. 38, 75
Jenny Johnson, *threeoclockbears.com* pp. 39, 111
Sandra Piper, *skyerosebears.com* pp. 37, 88
MaryAnn Wills, *maryannwillsexpressions.com* p. 85
Esther Lee, *estherbears.com* p. 81

The Baima Family
Bridget Crews
Jennifer Hacker

A Personal Note from the Author

Throughout the course of writing *Bear with Hope*—many hardships and heartaches have come our way. We lost our beloved miniature schnauzer Josie, to congestive heart failure. My dad suffered both a heart attack and gall bladder attack and was hospitalized for two weeks due to serious complications. My mother-in-law, Judy, was diagnosed with terminal breast cancer. Treatment was successful the first time, but the following year the cancer returned and the chemo was too much for Judy to endure. The cancer metastasized to her liver, bones, and lungs and quickly assaulted her body. Our family had planned to take her on a cruise, something Judy had anxiously and eagerly wanted to do. We were planning to cancel the trip due to her health, but she was adamant about going. Although her body was weak, her mind was strong and she insisted. With her doctor's blessing, and Judy's relentless determination to set sail with her family—on April 9, 2016 they boarded the ship. It would be a journey she would not return from. Judy passed away on the third day. As hard as it was witnessing the death of my own mother—it was likewise difficult seeing my husband and his family endure the death of their mom. It is heartbreaking not being able to make the pain go away for the ones you love. But it's not about making our pain go away; it's about making it through and past the pain. Whatever your struggles or sorrows, please know that there is hope, and there is light on the other side. It's okay to feel down and to feel frustrated and sad. Embrace your feelings, only be mindful of the thoughts that say you're not going to be happy or you aren't worthy—those thoughts you must learn to restore with hope and optimism. There is peace, joy and happiness for you; it's everywhere, and it's waiting for you to claim it as your own.

May you always, bear with hope.

Tammy

About the Author

Tammy graduated from the University of Oklahoma with a B.A. in psychology and a Master of Human Relations in counseling. This led her to a career in mental health and working with individuals affected by addiction, anxiety, depression, homelessness, schizoaffective and bi-polar disorders. Soon after the death of her mother, Tammy discovered a creative and therapeutic outlet by making memory teddy bears. Despite being born without a right forearm, Tammy put aside her chosen career in mental health and followed a new path, one that creatively offers comfort and hope in both the hands, and hearts of the hurting. Her unconventional means of creative visual and touch therapy has since evolved to help people who experience both human and pet loss. Her teddy bears and pet memorials have been featured in numerous television and print media within major industry publications across the globe. Now her full-time passion is creating memory bears and life-like dog memorials. Tammy lives in Oklahoma with her husband Marc, three miniature schnauzers and poodle.

Tammy's First Two Bears

Additional Reading and Resources

Course in Miracles, Foundation for Inner Peace

Life is Full of Sweet Spots: An Exploration of Joy, Mary O'Connor

Love is Letting Go of Fear, Gerald Jampolsky

Stolen Life: A Memoir, Jaycee Dugard

The Ultimate Caregiver, Bob Willis

When Bad Things Happen To Good People, Harold S. Kushner

Good Bears of the World, www.goodbearsoftheworld.org

Hope For The Day, suicide prevention, HFTD.org

Center for Help, centerforhelpandhope.org

Reagan Marie Teddy Bear Fund

MollyBears, *mollybears.com*

Grief Healing, a website to meet the needs of those who are mourning the loss of their loved ones, whether human or animal, www.griefhealing.com

Open to Hope Foundation is a non-profit foundation with the mission of helping people find hope after loss. www.opentohope.com

Crisis text hotline, www.crisistextline.org

Handmade memory bears, TammyBears.com and pet memorials, MyFureverFriend.com

References

Alvarsson, J. J., Wiens, S., & Nilsson, M. E. (2010). Stress Recovery during Exposure to Nature Sound and Environmental Noise. International Journal of Environmental Research and Public Health,7(3), 1036–1046. http://doi.org/10.3390/ijerph7031036

American Music Therapy Association. (2015)History of Music. Retrieved from http://www.musictherapy.org

Bell, C. & Robbins, S. (2007) Art Therapy. Journal of the American Art Therapy Association, 24 (2) p71-75

Bennett, M. P., & Lengacher, C. (2009). Humor and Laughter May Influence Health IV. Humor and Immune Function. Evidence-Based Complementary and Alternative Medicine Vol, 6(2), 159–164. http://doi.org/10.1093/ecam/nem149

Bradt, J., Drexel University (2011) Music interventions for improving psychological and physical outcomes in cancer patients. Cochrane Database of Systematic Reviews. Vol. 8

Bratman, G. (2015) Proceedings of the Natural Academy of Sciences. 112 (28):8567-72

Chadwick, M., Trewin, H., Gawthrop, F., & Wagstaff, C. (2013). Sesquiterpenoids Lactones: Benefits to Plants and People. International Journal of Molecular Sciences, 14(6), 12780–12805. http://doi.org/10.3390/ijms140612780

Department of Wildlife Conservation (2016) Immerse Yourself in a Forest for Better Health. Retrieved from: http://www.dec.ny.gov/lands/90720.html

Frankl, Viktor. (1959) Man's search for meaning. Boston, MA: Beacon Press

Group Health Research Institute. (2009) Depression and Anxiety. Retrieved from http://grouphealthresearch.org

Helsing, M. (2012) Everyday music listening: The importance of individual and situational factors for musical emotions and stress reduction. University of Gothenburg. Retrieved from http://hdl.handle.net/2077/28257

Llorens, L. (2012).Teddy bears accompany 35 percent of British adults to bed, survey says (poll). Huffington Post.

MacDonald, R. A. R. (2013). Music, health, and well-being: A review. *International Journal of Qualitative Studies on Health and Well-Being*, 8, 10.3402/qhw.v8io.20635. http://doi.org/10.3402/qhw.v8io.20635

Novotney, Amy (November 2013),Music as medicine. American Psychological Association Vol 44, No. 10 Retrieved from http://www.apa.org/monitor/2013/11/music.aspx

Rose, J. P., & Bartsch, H. H. (2009). Music as therapy. *Medicine and Music*, *70*, 5–8.

Sawyer, D. (2010) Jaycee Dugard: her first interview.

Retrieved from http://abcnews.go.com/US/abc-diane-sawyer-exclusive-jaycee-dugard-interview/story?id=13792803

Tai, K., et al. (2011) Touching a teddy bear mitigates the negative effects of social exclusion. Social Psychological and Personality Science. 2(6) , 618. National University of Singapore

University of Bristol. (April 2007)Getting dirt may lift your mood. Retrieved from:http://www.bristol.ac.uk/news/2007/5384.html

University of Maryland (2009) Laughter simply evokes an overall sense of well being. Retrieved from http://www.health.umd.edu/healthwellbeing

University of Maryland Medical Center (2008) Joyful music may promote heart health. Retrieved from http://www.umm.edu

University of Utah Pain Research Center (2011) *Journal of Pain*, Dec 12(12):1262-73

Van Den Berg, A.E., & Custers, M.H.(2010) Gardening promotes neuroendocrine and affective restoration from stress. J Health Psychol January 2011 vol. 16 no. 1 3-11 http://doi: 10.1177/1359105310365577

God grant me the serenity to accept the things I cannot change; courage to change the things I can; and wisdom to know the difference.